ADOM SON

MASTERING WEALTH CREATION

YOUR GUIDE TO FINANCIAL INDEPENDENCE: UNLOCK LASTING WEALTH AND FREEDOM

Copyright © 2024 by ADOM SON

All rights reserved. No part of this publication may be reproduced, stored or transmitted in any form or by any means, electronic, mechanical, photocopying, recording, scanning, or otherwise without written permission from the publisher. It is illegal to copy this book, post it to a website, or distribute it by any other means without permission.

ADOM SON asserts the moral right to be identified as the author of this work.

ADOM SON has no responsibility for the persistence or accuracy of URLs for external or third-party Internet Websites referred to in this publication and does not guarantee that any content on such Websites is, or will remain, accurate or appropriate.

Designations used by companies to distinguish their products are often claimed as trademarks. All brand names and product names used in this book and on its cover are trade names, service marks, trademarks and registered trademarks of their respective owners. The publishers and the book are not associated with any product or vendor mentioned in this book. None of the companies referenced within the book have endorsed the book.

First edition

This book was professionally typeset on Reedsy.
Find out more at reedsy.com

Contents

1	INTRODUCTION	1
2	Chapter 1: The Foundations of Wealth	3
3	Chapter 2: Income Streams	12
4	Chapter 3: Budgeting and Saving	21
5	Chapter 4: Investing Basics	31
6	Chapter 5: Advanced Investment Strategies	41
7	Chapter 6: Entrepreneurship and Wealth	51
8	Chapter 7: The Role of Technology in Wealth Creation	61
9	Chapter 8: Tax Planning and Wealth	71
10	Chapter 9: Wealth Preservation	80
11	Chapter 10: The Psychology of Wealth	90
12	Chapter 11: Networking and Wealth	99
13	Chapter 12: Philanthropy and Giving Back	109
14	Chapter 13: Adapting to Economic Changes	118
15	Chapter 14: The Journey to Mastery	128
16	RECOMMENDED BOOKS	137

1

INTRODUCTION

As we reach the culmination of 'Mastering Wealth Creation: Your Guide to Financial Independence,' it is essential to reflect on the transformative insights and practical strategies explored throughout this book. The path to financial independence is not merely a series of steps but a continuous evolution of mindset, knowledge, and action. Each chapter has provided a roadmap to understanding the intricacies of wealth creation, equipping you with the tools necessary to unlock lasting prosperity and freedom.

The principles discussed are designed to empower you to take control of your financial destiny. By applying the techniques of budgeting, investing, and financial planning, you have the foundation to build a secure and prosperous future. The emphasis on discipline, patience, and informed decision-making underscores the reality that wealth is not an overnight achievement but a lifelong commitment to growth and learning.

It is important to remember that financial independence is

deeply personal, varying with each individual's goals, values, and circumstances. The strategies within these pages encourage you to tailor your approach to wealth creation, ensuring it aligns with your unique vision of success. As you continue on this path, remain open to adapting your strategies as your life evolves and new opportunities arise.

The journey to financial independence is both challenging and rewarding, requiring resilience and determination. Through perseverance and the application of the knowledge gained here, you can achieve a level of financial freedom that enhances not only your life but also the lives of those around you. The pursuit of wealth creation is not solely about monetary gain; it is about creating a life of purpose, fulfillment, and security.

May this book serve as a lasting resource, inspiring you to reach new heights in your financial endeavors. As you forge ahead, let the principles of wisdom, integrity, and innovation guide you towards a future of abundance and freedom.

Chapter 1: The Foundations of Wealth

UNDERSTANDING WEALTH

In the intricate tapestry of human civilization, wealth has always held a pivotal role. It is a concept that transcends mere numbers in a bank account, enveloping a broader spectrum of values, assets, and resources. The essence of wealth lies not only in its tangibility but also in its profound impact on one's quality of life, opportunities, and the ability to influence the world. Historically, wealth has been a driving force behind societal progress, technological advancements, and cultural development.

At its core, wealth is often perceived as financial prosperity, an accumulation of money and material possessions. However, this perspective only scratches the surface of its true nature. Wealth encompasses a variety of facets including emotional, social, intellectual, and spiritual dimensions. It provides security, comfort, and the freedom to pursue one's passions and dreams.

The multidimensional nature of wealth means it is both a means and an end, a tool for achieving personal and communal goals.

Understanding wealth requires a deep dive into the paradigms that shape our perception of it. Cultural, economic, and philosophical influences play significant roles in defining what wealth means to different individuals and societies. In some cultures, wealth is measured by the richness of relationships, communal harmony, and the abundance of natural resources. In others, it is quantified by economic indicators, investment portfolios, and financial independence.

The journey to mastering wealth creation begins with a shift in mindset. It involves recognizing that wealth is not solely about accumulation but about creating value. This creation of value can manifest in various forms, such as generating innovative ideas, nurturing talents, or contributing to societal well-being. True wealth is sustainable and regenerative, benefiting not only the individual but also the larger community.

In the modern world, the concept of wealth is continually evolving. The digital age has introduced new forms of wealth such as digital currencies, intellectual property, and online platforms that democratize access to opportunities. The ability to leverage technology, information, and networks has become a crucial determinant of wealth in today's interconnected global economy.

Moreover, understanding wealth involves acknowledging the responsibilities it entails. With great wealth comes the power to effect change, and with that power comes the responsibility to use it wisely and ethically. Philanthropy and responsible investing are avenues through which individuals and organizations can contribute to a more equitable and sustainable world.

In essence, the mastery of wealth creation is an ongoing process of learning, adapting, and growing. It requires a balance between ambition and contentment, between acquiring and giving, and between personal success and collective progress. As individuals seek to understand and harness the power of wealth, they inevitably contribute to shaping a future where prosperity is accessible to all, and wealth, in its truest sense, enriches the human experience.

THE MINDSET OF ABUNDANCE

In the realm of wealth creation, the mindset one cultivates can be as critical as the strategies employed. This chapter delves into the mindset of abundance, a perspective that transcends mere financial accumulation and enters the domain of limitless possibilities. To truly understand this mindset, one must first recognize its foundation: the belief that the world is teeming with opportunities, resources, and potential for everyone. This belief is not just optimistic thinking; it is a lens through which successful individuals perceive the world, enabling them to spot opportunities where others see only scarcity.

An abundance mindset is characterized by a profound sense of gratitude and contentment. Individuals with this mindset appreciate what they have while remaining open to receiving more. They understand that wealth is not a finite resource but an ever-expanding entity that grows with sharing and collaboration. This perspective encourages generosity and fosters a community where ideas and resources circulate freely, creating a synergistic environment where everyone can thrive.

Central to this mindset is the principle of expansion rather than contraction. People with an abundant mindset focus on growth, both personally and professionally. They invest in learning, continuously seeking knowledge and skills to enhance their capabilities. This growth-oriented approach not only amplifies their potential to acquire wealth but also enriches their lives with diverse experiences and insights.

Moreover, the mindset of abundance involves a shift from competitive to collaborative thinking. Instead of viewing others as rivals, individuals with this mindset see them as potential partners and collaborators. This shift in perspective opens the door to partnerships, joint ventures, and shared successes, creating a network of support that can prove invaluable in any wealth creation journey.

Another crucial element of this mindset is resilience. Believing in abundance instills a sense of confidence and security, empowering individuals to take calculated risks. They understand that setbacks are not the end but rather stepping stones to greater achievements. This resilience is rooted in the conviction that every challenge brings with it a lesson and an opportunity for growth.

The mindset of abundance also fosters a long-term perspective. Individuals who adopt this view focus on sustainable growth rather than immediate gains. They are patient, understanding that true wealth accumulates over time through consistent effort and smart investments. This long-term vision allows them to make decisions that benefit not only their immediate circumstances but also their future prosperity.

Ultimately, cultivating an abundance mindset requires intentional effort and practice. It involves consciously choosing to view the world through a lens of possibilities rather than limitations. By doing so, individuals unlock a wealth of opportunities that might otherwise remain hidden. In the pursuit of mastering wealth creation, adopting this mindset is not merely advantageous; it is transformative, paving the way for a life rich in both material and intangible wealth. Through the power of an abundant mindset, the journey to wealth becomes not just a means to an end but a rewarding and fulfilling experience in itself.

SETTING FINANCIAL GOALS

At the heart of every successful financial strategy lies the art of setting clear, actionable goals. These goals serve as the compass guiding one's journey through the vast landscape of wealth creation. To craft these goals, one must first delve deep into personal aspirations and financial dreams, transforming abstract desires into tangible targets. This process requires introspection and a keen understanding of one's current financial standing.

The initial step in this transformative process involves identifying what truly matters. This could range from ensuring a comfortable retirement, purchasing a dream home, funding a child's education, or perhaps achieving financial independence. Each goal, no matter its nature, must be specific and well-defined, for vague ambitions often lead to uncertain paths.

Once these aspirations are delineated, the next crucial phase is to quantify them. Assigning a monetary value and a timeline to each goal is essential. This not only provides a clear target but also introduces a sense of urgency and purpose. For instance, if the aim is to accumulate a certain sum by retirement, one must calculate the monthly savings required, taking into account variables like inflation and expected returns on investment.

A pivotal aspect of setting financial goals is prioritization. With numerous aspirations competing for limited resources, it's vital to rank them based on urgency and importance. This hierarchy ensures that essential goals receive the focus and resources they deserve. For example, an emergency fund might take precedence over a luxury vacation, given its role in safeguarding against unforeseen financial setbacks.

Moreover, flexibility is an indispensable component of effective goal-setting. Life is unpredictable, and circumstances can shift rapidly. Thus, while goals should be steadfast, the strategies to achieve them must be adaptable. Regularly revisiting and adjusting these goals in response to life changes, such as career shifts, family expansions, or economic fluctuations, ensures they remain relevant and achievable.

An often-overlooked element in this process is the psychological impact of goal-setting. Achieving financial milestones can significantly boost one's confidence and motivation, creating a positive feedback loop that propels further progress. Conversely, setting unrealistic goals can lead to frustration and disillusionment. Therefore, while ambition is crucial, it must be balanced with realism.

Furthermore, the act of writing down financial goals can enhance commitment and accountability. Documenting these targets serves as a constant reminder of one's financial aspirations, making it easier to resist temptations that might derail progress. Sharing these goals with a trusted advisor or partner can also provide an additional layer of accountability, fostering a supportive environment conducive to success.

In essence, setting financial goals is about more than just numbers. It's a dynamic, ongoing process that intertwines with personal values and life aspirations. By meticulously defining, quantifying, and prioritizing these goals, while remaining adaptable and realistic, individuals can chart a course towards financial prosperity that is both purposeful and fulfilling. This strategic approach not only unlocks the potential for wealth creation but also instills a profound sense of financial empowerment and peace of mind.

THE IMPORTANCE OF FINANCIAL EDUCATION

In the modern financial landscape, the role of financial education has emerged as a pivotal element in the journey of wealth creation. A comprehensive understanding of financial principles is not merely a luxury but a necessity for anyone aspiring to achieve financial independence and security. This knowledge serves as the foundation upon which individuals can build a prosperous future, enabling them to make informed decisions, mitigate risks, and seize opportunities that may otherwise remain hidden.

At its core, financial education equips individuals with the tools to navigate the complexities of personal finance. It encompasses a wide range of topics, from budgeting and saving to investing and retirement planning. By understanding these concepts, individuals gain the confidence to manage their finances effectively, ensuring that they are prepared for both expected and unforeseen financial challenges. This preparation is crucial in a world where economic uncertainties can quickly derail even the most carefully laid plans.

One of the key benefits of financial education is its ability to demystify the world of investing. With a solid grasp of investment principles, individuals can move beyond the fear and apprehension often associated with stock markets and other financial instruments. They learn to analyze risks, understand market trends, and develop strategies that align with their financial goals. This empowerment transforms investing from a daunting task into an opportunity for growth and wealth accumulation.

Moreover, financial education fosters a mindset of proactive financial management. It encourages individuals to take charge of their financial future rather than leaving it to chance or relying solely on external advisors. By acquiring knowledge about tax planning, debt management, and insurance, individuals can optimize their financial decisions and maximize their resources. This proactive approach not only enhances personal financial well-being but also contributes to broader economic stability as more people become financially literate and capable of making sound economic choices.

The significance of financial education extends beyond personal gain; it has profound implications for society as a whole. Financially educated individuals are better equipped to contribute to their communities, support local economies, and participate in philanthropic endeavors. They are also more likely to advocate for policies that promote financial literacy and inclusion, creating a ripple effect that benefits future generations.

In an era where financial products and services are becoming increasingly complex, the importance of financial education cannot be overstated. It serves as a critical tool for leveling the playing field, enabling individuals from all walks of life to access opportunities that can lead to financial security and prosperity. By prioritizing financial education, we can build a more equitable and financially resilient society.

Ultimately, the value of financial education lies in its ability to transform lives. It empowers individuals to break free from the constraints of financial ignorance and unlock their potential to create, sustain, and grow wealth. As more people embrace the principles of financial education, they will be better positioned to achieve their aspirations and contribute to a thriving global economy.

3

Chapter 2: Income Streams

ACTIVE VS PASSIVE INCOME

In the landscape of wealth creation, understanding the distinction between active and passive income is fundamental. Active income is the earnings derived from direct involvement in work or services. This form of income is typically generated through salaries, wages, commissions, and tips. It is the result of trading time and effort for money, where the individual plays a central role in the income-generating process. For example, a lawyer billing hours, a doctor attending to patients, or a salesperson earning through commissions all rely on active income. The primary characteristic of active income is its direct link to effort; if the effort ceases, so does the income.

On the other hand, passive income flows in with minimal active involvement once the initial setup is complete. This form of income is generated through investments, rental properties, royalties, or business endeavors that do not require daily attention. The essence of passive income lies in its ability to generate earnings without the need for continuous active participation. For instance, a landlord receives rent payments from tenants, an author earns royalties from book sales, and an investor collects dividends from stocks.

The allure of passive income is its potential to provide financial freedom and time flexibility. It allows individuals to detach their earnings from the constraints of time, offering the possibility of earning while pursuing other interests or even while sleeping. This detachment is what makes passive income a cornerstone in the pursuit of wealth creation.

However, the journey to establishing passive income streams is often paved with initial active efforts and investments. Building a successful passive income source requires strategic planning, significant upfront investment, and sometimes years of nurturing before it becomes self-sustaining. For example, investing in real estate might require substantial capital and management before it consistently generates rental income.

The distinction between active and passive income also reflects in tax implications. Typically, active income is subject to higher tax rates compared to passive income. This difference emphasizes the importance of diversifying income streams for tax efficiency and wealth accumulation.

In the broader context of personal finance, the balance between active and passive income can significantly impact one's financial security and lifestyle choices. Relying solely on active income can be risky, especially in unpredictable economic climates or personal life changes. Diversifying income sources by incorporating passive streams offers a buffer against financial uncertainties.

Thus, understanding and leveraging both active and passive income is crucial for individuals aiming to master wealth creation. It requires a mindful assessment of one's skills, resources, and long-term financial goals. While active income provides immediate financial support, cultivating passive income paves the way for sustained wealth and financial independence. This harmonious balance is key to unlocking a financially secure future.

BUILDING MULTIPLE INCOME STREAMS

The concept of diversifying income streams is akin to weaving a rich tapestry of financial security and growth. It involves strategically layering multiple sources of revenue, each contributing to a robust financial portfolio, much like the intricate threads in a finely crafted fabric. This approach not only fortifies one's financial foundation but also offers resilience against economic fluctuations and unforeseen life events.

Imagine a life where one is not solely reliant on a single paycheck. Instead, there are various channels through which money flows, each with its distinct rhythm and reliability. This multiplicity of income sources can include investments in stocks, bonds, or real estate, alongside entrepreneurial ventures or freelance projects that leverage personal skills and passions. The beauty of this strategy lies in its versatility and adaptability, allowing individuals to tailor their income streams to fit their unique lifestyles and financial goals.

Real estate, for instance, can serve as a tangible and lucrative income stream. By investing in rental properties, individuals can generate a steady flow of passive income. The key is to identify properties in thriving locations, where demand is high, ensuring consistent occupancy and returns. Moreover, the appreciation of real estate over time can significantly enhance one's net worth, providing both immediate and long-term financial benefits.

Similarly, the stock market offers a plethora of opportunities for wealth creation. By investing in a diversified portfolio of stocks and bonds, individuals can benefit from capital gains and dividends. This requires a keen understanding of market trends and an ability to make informed investment decisions. The advent of technology has also democratized access to the stock market, allowing even novice investors to participate and grow their wealth.

Entrepreneurial ventures represent another vital income stream. Whether launching a startup or engaging in side hustles, entrepreneurship allows individuals to capitalize on their talents and interests. This not only generates income but also fosters personal growth and satisfaction. The digital age has further expanded these opportunities, with online businesses and e-commerce platforms providing accessible avenues for aspiring entrepreneurs.

Freelancing and consulting work offer additional avenues for income diversification. By leveraging professional expertise, individuals can offer services on a project basis, often commanding higher rates than traditional employment. This flexibility enables individuals to work on their terms, balancing multiple projects and maximizing earning potential.

The essence of building multiple income streams lies in its proactive nature. It requires a mindset shift from passive reliance on a single source of income to an active pursuit of financial independence. This approach encourages continuous learning and adaptation, as individuals explore new opportunities and refine their strategies. By cultivating a diverse portfolio of income streams, one not only enhances their financial security but also gains the freedom to pursue personal and professional aspirations with confidence and ease.

INVESTING IN REAL ESTATE

Real estate investment stands as a cornerstone in the realm of wealth creation, offering a tangible asset that can appreciate over time while providing the potential for steady income. It is a field where patience and strategic foresight can yield significant returns, making it an attractive option for both seasoned investors and newcomers alike. The allure of real estate lies not only in its potential for capital growth but also in its ability to generate passive income, serving as a hedge against inflation and market volatility.

The world of real estate is vast and varied, encompassing a range of opportunities from residential properties to commercial spaces, and from undeveloped land to industrial units. Each type of investment comes with its own set of risks and rewards, requiring a deep understanding of market dynamics and economic indicators. Residential properties, for example, offer the benefit of a broad market appeal and consistent demand. However, they also come with the challenges of tenant management and property maintenance.

Commercial real estate, on the other hand, can provide higher yields and longer lease terms, but often requires a more substantial initial investment and a keen understanding of business cycles. Investing in commercial properties demands a thorough analysis of location, tenant quality, and lease terms, as these factors can significantly influence the profitability of the investment.

One of the critical aspects of investing in real estate is location. The adage "location, location, location" holds true, as the value of a property is intrinsically linked to its geographical placement. Proximity to amenities, schools, transportation, and employment centers can dramatically affect property values and rental income potential. Investors must conduct comprehensive market research to identify areas poised for growth and development.

Financing is another pivotal element in real estate investment. Leveraging borrowed capital can amplify returns, but it also introduces additional risk. Understanding the nuances of mortgage rates, loan terms, and financing options is crucial for maximizing profitability while managing debt responsibly. Investors should also be aware of the tax implications associated with real estate investments, as these can impact overall returns.

Diversification within a real estate portfolio can mitigate risk and enhance stability. By spreading investments across different property types and geographic locations, investors can protect themselves against market fluctuations and economic downturns. This strategy requires a balance of risk tolerance and investment goals, ensuring that the portfolio aligns with the investor's financial objectives.

The journey of investing in real estate is as much about personal growth as it is about financial gain. It demands a willingness to learn, adapt, and respond to market changes. Building a network of industry professionals, including real estate agents, property managers, and financial advisors, can provide valuable insights and support. Staying informed about market trends, economic forecasts, and regulatory changes is essential for making informed investment decisions.

In the ever-evolving landscape of wealth creation, real estate remains a steadfast pillar, offering opportunities for growth and security. It is a field where diligent research, strategic planning, and prudent financial management can pave the way to enduring prosperity.

INVESTING IN STOCKS

In the intricate tapestry of wealth creation, the stock market stands as a vibrant and dynamic thread, offering opportunities for growth and prosperity. It is a realm where fortunes are built, sometimes lost, and often regained, through the strategic allocation of resources into publicly traded companies. For the discerning investor, understanding the nuances of stock investing is paramount to mastering the art of wealth creation.

Stocks, representing ownership shares in a company, are a fundamental component of any diversified investment portfolio. They offer the potential for both capital appreciation and dividend income, making them an attractive option for those seeking to grow their wealth over time. The stock market is characterized by its volatility, where prices fluctuate based on a myriad of factors including economic indicators, corporate performance, geopolitical events, and investor sentiment.

To navigate this complex landscape, investors must equip themselves with a robust understanding of market fundamentals. This begins with analyzing financial statements, which provide insight into a company's health and performance. Key metrics such as earnings per share (EPS), price-to-earnings (P/E) ratio, and return on equity (ROE) serve as vital indicators of a company's profitability and efficiency. Investors must also stay informed about broader economic trends that may impact market conditions, such as interest rates, inflation, and employment figures.

Diversification is a critical strategy in minimizing risk and maximizing returns. By spreading investments across various sectors and industries, investors can mitigate the impact of market volatility. This approach reduces the risk associated with any single stock or sector downturn, ensuring a more stable portfolio performance. Additionally, understanding the distinction between growth and value stocks can aid in constructing a balanced portfolio. Growth stocks, typically characterized by higher potential for price appreciation, may offer substantial returns but often come with increased risk. Conversely, value stocks, often undervalued by the market, provide opportunities for steady returns with potentially lower risk.

Moreover, the role of technology in stock investing cannot be overstated. With the advent of online trading platforms and financial technologies, investors have unprecedented access to real-time data, research tools, and investment opportunities. This democratization of information empowers individuals to make informed decisions, leveling the playing field between individual and institutional investors.

However, investing in stocks requires more than just technical knowledge. It demands discipline, patience, and a long-term perspective. Emotional resilience is crucial, as markets can be unpredictable and investor psychology often drives market trends. The ability to remain steadfast during market downturns, avoiding the temptation to sell in panic, is a hallmark of successful investors.

Ultimately, investing in stocks is an art as much as it is a science. It is about making informed decisions based on thorough research and analysis while balancing risk and reward. As investors delve into the stock market, they embark on a journey toward financial growth, armed with the knowledge and tools to navigate the ever-changing landscape of wealth creation.

4

Chapter 3: Budgeting and Saving

CREATING A BUDGET

In the realm of wealth creation, the cornerstone of financial success is the meticulous crafting of a budget. This fundamental process is akin to laying the foundation of a grand architectural masterpiece, where each element meticulously aligns to support the grand vision. A budget is not merely a list of numbers; it is a strategic blueprint that guides financial decisions and shapes the path to economic prosperity.

The initial step in creating a budget involves a comprehensive assessment of one's financial landscape. This requires an honest and thorough evaluation of income streams, encompassing not only salaries but also dividends, rental income, or any other sources. Understanding the complete picture of income is crucial, as it sets the parameters within which financial decisions will be made.

Equally important is the cataloging of expenses, which demands a keen eye for detail. This process involves distinguishing between fixed and variable expenses. Fixed expenses, such as mortgage payments or car loans, are predictable and consistent, while variable expenses, like groceries or entertainment, can fluctuate. Recognizing this distinction is vital for identifying areas where adjustments can be made to optimize financial health.

A well-crafted budget also considers the future, incorporating savings and investment goals as integral components. Allocating a portion of income towards savings ensures a safety net for unforeseen circumstances, while investments serve as the engine for wealth growth. This forward-thinking approach necessitates setting realistic goals, whether it be building an emergency fund, saving for retirement, or investing in stocks. Each goal should be specific, measurable, and time-bound, providing clear targets to strive for.

Technology can be an invaluable ally in this endeavor. Budgeting apps and financial software offer tools to track expenses, set reminders for bill payments, and analyze spending patterns. These digital aids can transform the budgeting process from a tedious chore into an engaging and insightful activity. They offer visualizations that make it easier to understand complex financial data, enabling informed decision-making.

Creating a budget is not a one-time task but an evolving process. It requires regular review and adjustment to reflect changes in income, expenses, or financial goals. This dynamic nature ensures that the budget remains relevant and effective, adapting to life's inevitable fluctuations. It is a living document that grows alongside the individual's financial journey, providing guidance and clarity.

Moreover, the psychological aspect of budgeting cannot be overlooked. It instills discipline and fosters a sense of control over one's financial destiny. This empowerment can reduce stress and anxiety related to money matters, promoting a healthier relationship with finances. By adhering to a budget, individuals can break free from the cycle of living paycheck to paycheck, paving the way for long-term wealth accumulation.

In essence, creating a budget is an art form that combines analytical precision with visionary planning. It requires patience, discipline, and a commitment to financial literacy. As the bedrock of wealth creation, a well-constructed budget not only organizes finances but also inspires confidence, setting the stage for a prosperous future.

SAVING STRATEGIES

In the intricate tapestry of wealth creation, the art of saving emerges as a foundational thread, weaving stability and potential into one's financial life. At the heart of this practice lies the ability to balance present desires with future aspirations, creating a harmonious relationship between income and expenditure. Saving effectively requires more than just setting aside money; it demands a strategic approach that aligns with one's long-term financial goals.

The first step in developing a robust saving strategy involves understanding the significance of setting clear and achievable goals. Whether these goals pertain to purchasing a home, funding education, or ensuring a comfortable retirement, they serve as a compass, directing the flow of financial resources. By establishing specific targets, individuals can cultivate discipline and motivation, transforming saving from a mundane task into a purposeful endeavor.

A crucial component of successful saving strategies is the adoption of a systematic approach. Automating savings can significantly enhance consistency and reduce the temptation to spend impulsively. By directing a fixed percentage of income into savings accounts or investment vehicles automatically, individuals can effortlessly build their wealth over time. This method not only simplifies the saving process but also takes advantage of the power of compounding, where interest earns additional interest, amplifying the growth of savings.

Diversification within saving strategies further strengthens financial security. Allocating funds across different types of accounts—such as high-yield savings accounts, certificates of deposit, and retirement accounts—offers a balance of accessibility and growth potential. Each type of account serves a specific purpose, providing liquidity for short-term needs and growth for long-term objectives. This diversified approach ensures that savings are not only protected but also positioned to benefit from varying economic conditions.

The role of budgeting cannot be overstated when crafting effective saving strategies. By meticulously tracking income and expenses, individuals gain insight into their financial habits and identify areas for improvement. This awareness enables the creation of a realistic budget that prioritizes saving without compromising essential living expenses. A well-structured budget acts as a roadmap, guiding financial decisions and ensuring that savings remain a priority.

Moreover, the importance of emergency funds cannot be overlooked. Establishing a financial cushion to cover unexpected expenses—such as medical emergencies or sudden job loss—prevents the need to dip into long-term savings, preserving the integrity of one's financial strategy. Typically, an emergency fund should cover three to six months of living expenses, offering peace of mind and financial resilience.

Finally, adaptability is a hallmark of effective saving strategies. As life circumstances evolve, so too should one's approach to saving. Regularly reviewing and adjusting saving plans in response to changes in income, expenses, or financial goals ensures continued alignment with one's overarching wealth creation strategy. This flexibility allows individuals to navigate life's uncertainties while maintaining progress toward their financial aspirations.

In the realm of wealth creation, saving strategies serve as a cornerstone, providing the stability and security necessary to capitalize on future opportunities. By embracing a thoughtful and disciplined approach to saving, individuals can lay a solid foundation for financial success, transforming their aspirations into tangible realities.

EMERGENCY FUNDS

In the vast landscape of personal finance, the concept of an emergency fund stands as a steadfast pillar, offering both security and peace of mind. Picture it as a financial safety net, meticulously woven to catch you in times of unforeseen circumstances. An emergency fund is a reservoir of readily accessible cash, set aside to navigate life's unpredictable challenges. It is not a mere luxury, but a fundamental component of sound financial planning, ensuring that unexpected events do not derail your long-term financial goals.

Imagine the sudden loss of a job, an urgent medical expense, or an unexpected home repair. These events, while unpredictable, are part of the ebb and flow of life. Without an emergency fund, such occurrences can lead to financial turmoil, forcing individuals to rely on high-interest debt or deplete their long-term savings. The purpose of an emergency fund is to provide a buffer, allowing you to handle these situations with a level of financial grace and stability.

The size of an emergency fund is a topic of much discussion among financial experts, but the consensus is that it should cover three to six months' worth of living expenses. This range offers a balance between providing adequate coverage for most emergencies and maintaining liquidity. The exact amount, however, depends on individual circumstances such as job stability, income level, and personal comfort with risk. A single-income household might aim for six months of expenses, whereas a dual-income family might find three months sufficient.

Building an emergency fund is a process that requires discipline and foresight. It begins with setting a clear goal based on your monthly expenses and then devising a plan to reach it. This might involve setting aside a certain percentage of your income each month or reallocating funds from non-essential expenses. The key is consistency and commitment, ensuring that the fund grows steadily over time.

The placement of your emergency fund is equally important. It should be kept in a highly liquid account, such as a savings account or money market account, where it can be accessed quickly without penalties or delays. While it may be tempting to invest this money for higher returns, the primary objective of an emergency fund is accessibility and security, not growth.

An emergency fund is not only a financial tool but also a psychological one. It provides a sense of control and preparedness, reducing stress and anxiety associated with financial uncertainty. Knowing that you have a cushion to fall back on can enhance your overall financial confidence, allowing you to make decisions from a position of strength rather than fear.

In the broader context of wealth creation, an emergency fund serves as a foundational element. It protects your investments and long-term savings from being tapped into during crises, allowing them to continue growing unabated. By safeguarding your financial future against the unexpected, an emergency fund is a testament to prudent financial management and a crucial step in mastering wealth creation.

DEBT MANAGEMENT

Navigating the complex landscape of debt management requires a strategic balance between leveraging financial opportunities and mitigating potential risks. In the pursuit of wealth creation, understanding how to effectively manage debt is crucial. Debt, when handled wisely, can serve as a powerful tool to accelerate growth and enhance financial stability. However, mismanagement can lead to a cascade of negative consequences, potentially derailing one's financial objectives.

Effective debt management begins with a comprehensive assessment of one's financial situation. This involves identifying all existing liabilities, including credit card balances, personal loans, mortgages, and any other financial obligations. An accurate picture of total debt allows for the development of a structured plan to address each component systematically. Prioritizing debts based on interest rates and terms is a prudent step, as it enables individuals to focus on paying off high-interest debts first, thereby reducing the overall financial burden.

Budgeting plays a pivotal role in debt management. Establishing a realistic budget that aligns with one's income and expenses is essential for maintaining control over finances. A well-structured budget not only ensures timely debt repayments but also facilitates the allocation of funds towards savings and investments. By consistently adhering to a budget, individuals can gradually reduce their debt load while simultaneously building a financial cushion for future needs.

Another critical aspect of debt management is understanding the nuances of interest rates and loan terms. Negotiating better terms with creditors can significantly impact the cost of borrowing. Refinancing options, such as consolidating high-interest debts into a lower-interest loan, can provide relief and simplify repayment processes. Additionally, exploring balance transfer opportunities with credit cards may offer temporary interest-free periods, allowing for more focused debt reduction efforts.

The psychological component of debt management should not be overlooked. Debt can be a source of significant stress and anxiety, affecting both mental health and overall well-being. Developing a positive mindset towards debt, viewing it as a challenge to overcome rather than an insurmountable obstacle, can motivate individuals to remain disciplined in their financial practices. Seeking support from financial advisors or counselors can also provide valuable insights and emotional reassurance.

Moreover, cultivating financial literacy is imperative in mastering debt management. Understanding the intricacies of different types of debt, credit scores, and financial products empowers individuals to make informed decisions. Continuous education in financial matters equips individuals with the knowledge to navigate complex financial landscapes and anticipate potential challenges.

In the broader context of wealth creation, debt management is not merely about eliminating liabilities but rather about strategically utilizing debt to achieve financial goals. When used judiciously, debt can facilitate investments in education, property, and business ventures, ultimately contributing to long-term wealth accumulation. The key lies in maintaining a delicate balance—leveraging debt to seize opportunities while ensuring that repayment obligations remain manageable.

By adopting a proactive and informed approach to debt management, individuals can transform debt from a potential hindrance into a catalyst for financial growth. The journey towards mastering wealth creation is significantly enhanced when debt is harnessed effectively, paving the way for a secure and prosperous financial future.

5

Chapter 4: Investing Basics

UNDERSTANDING RISK AND REWARD

In the intricate tapestry of wealth creation, an understanding of the delicate balance between risk and reward serves as a cornerstone for those aspiring to financial mastery. This fundamental concept is not merely an abstract notion but a practical guide that influences every decision an investor makes. At its core, risk is the potential for loss, an inherent uncertainty that accompanies any investment. Reward, conversely, is the potential for gain, the enticing prospect that fuels the pursuit of financial growth.

In financial markets, the relationship between risk and reward is symbiotic, each necessitating the other in a dance that defines investment strategies. Higher potential rewards often come with increased levels of risk, a principle that shapes the decisions of seasoned investors. The challenge lies in identifying the optimal point where the promise of reward justifies the acceptance of risk, a task that requires keen insight and strategic acumen.

Risk manifests in various forms, each with its own implications. Market risk, for instance, is the possibility of losses due to factors that affect the entire market, such as economic recessions or political instability. Credit risk involves the likelihood that a borrower will default on their obligations, while liquidity risk pertains to the difficulty of converting assets into cash without significant loss. Each type of risk demands careful consideration, as the impact can ripple through an investment portfolio, affecting overall performance.

Investors, therefore, must cultivate a nuanced understanding of these risks and develop strategies to mitigate them. Diversification, often touted as a key risk management tool, involves spreading investments across different asset classes to reduce exposure to any single risk. By not putting all their eggs in one basket, investors can cushion themselves against market volatility and unforeseen downturns.

The art of balancing risk and reward also involves an introspective component—understanding one's own risk tolerance. This personal threshold for risk, influenced by factors such as age, financial goals, and emotional temperament, plays a crucial role in shaping investment decisions. A young investor with a long time horizon might be more inclined to take on higher-risk opportunities for greater potential returns. In contrast, someone nearing retirement may prioritize preserving capital over aggressive growth.

Furthermore, the evolving landscape of financial markets demands that investors remain vigilant and adaptable. Technological advancements, regulatory changes, and global events continuously reshape the risk-reward paradigm, requiring a dynamic approach to investment strategies. Staying informed and educated about these shifts enables investors to make informed decisions that align with their financial objectives.

Ultimately, mastering the interplay between risk and reward is not about eliminating risk entirely—an impossible feat—but about managing it effectively. It involves a strategic approach that combines knowledge, experience, and intuition to navigate the complexities of the financial world. By understanding the intricate dynamics of risk and reward, investors can position themselves to seize opportunities while safeguarding their financial future, laying a solid foundation for wealth creation.

TYPES OF INVESTMENTS

In the vast landscape of wealth creation, navigating through the myriad options of investments can seem daunting. Yet, understanding the types of investments is crucial for building a diversified portfolio that aligns with one's financial goals and risk tolerance. Investments can be broadly categorized into several types, each offering distinct characteristics, potential returns, and risks.

Equities, or stocks, represent ownership in a company and are one of the most common types of investments. When you purchase stocks, you essentially buy a piece of the company, and your return is tied to the company's performance. Equities are known for their high-risk, high-reward potential. They can offer substantial returns through capital appreciation and dividends, but they are also subject to market volatility and economic fluctuations.

Bonds are another foundational investment type. These are essentially loans made to a corporation or government entity, with the promise of repayment with interest over a specified period. Bonds are generally considered safer than stocks, offering more predictable returns and lower risk. However, they may also provide lower returns compared to equities. They are an attractive option for conservative investors seeking steady income and preservation of capital.

Real estate investments involve purchasing properties for rental income or capital appreciation. Real estate can be a tangible asset that not only provides potential rental income but also appreciates in value over time. It offers diversification benefits and can serve as a hedge against inflation. However, investing in real estate requires significant capital and can involve complexities such as property management and market fluctuations.

Mutual funds and exchange-traded funds (ETFs) offer another avenue for investment. These funds pool money from multiple investors to purchase a diversified portfolio of stocks, bonds, or other securities. Managed by professional fund managers, mutual funds and ETFs provide investors with diversification, liquidity, and professional management. They are suitable for those who prefer a hands-off approach to investing.

Commodities, including precious metals like gold and silver, agricultural products, and energy resources, provide another investment opportunity. These tangible assets are often used as a hedge against inflation and currency fluctuations. Commodities can be volatile and are influenced by supply and demand dynamics, geopolitical events, and natural disasters.

Cryptocurrencies have emerged as a modern type of investment, characterized by digital assets like Bitcoin and Ethereum. Known for their volatility, cryptocurrencies offer high-risk, high-reward potential. They are decentralized and offer diversification benefits, but they also come with regulatory uncertainties and technological risks.

Finally, alternative investments encompass a broad category that includes hedge funds, private equity, and venture capital. These investments are typically available to accredited investors and involve strategies that go beyond traditional stock and bond investments. They offer the potential for high returns but come with higher risks and lower liquidity.

Understanding these types of investments is essential for crafting a strategy that suits individual financial goals. Each type offers unique benefits and challenges, and selecting the right mix can enhance wealth creation while managing risk effectively.

DIVERSIFICATION

In the realm of wealth creation, the concept of diversification stands as a pillar of prudent financial strategy. Diversification involves spreading investments across various financial instruments, industries, and other categories to reduce exposure to risk. By allocating investments among different financial vehicles, an investor can mitigate the adverse effects of market volatility and unforeseen economic downturns. The goal is to maximize returns by investing in different areas that would each react differently to the same event.

The principle of diversification is rooted in the idea that a well-diversified portfolio will, on average, yield higher returns and pose a lower risk than any individual investment found within the portfolio. This is because the positive performance of some investments will neutralize the negative performance of others. The practice is akin to not putting all one's eggs in a single basket, thereby safeguarding one's assets against the unpredictability of financial markets.

Diversification can be achieved in several ways. One common approach is through asset allocation, which involves dividing an investment portfolio among different asset categories, such as stocks, bonds, and cash. Each asset class has different levels of risk and return, so each will behave differently over time. For instance, when stocks perform poorly, bonds may perform well, thus balancing the portfolio's overall performance.

Another method is geographic diversification, which spreads investments across various countries and regions. This approach helps to protect against country-specific risks, such as political instability or economic recessions. By investing in international markets, investors can benefit from growth in emerging economies and currency fluctuations that may favor foreign investments.

Industry diversification is also crucial, as it involves investing in different sectors of the economy. For example, an investor might allocate funds across technology, healthcare, and consumer goods sectors. This strategy ensures that the portfolio is not overly exposed to the downturns of any single industry, which can be caused by regulatory changes, technological innovations, or shifts in consumer preferences.

Furthermore, diversification can extend to different types of securities within the same asset class. For example, within the stock category, an investor might spread investments across large-cap, mid-cap, and small-cap stocks. Similarly, in the bond category, one might invest in government bonds, municipal bonds, and corporate bonds.

While diversification is a powerful tool for managing risk, it does not guarantee profits or protect against losses in a declining market. It is essential to periodically review and adjust the portfolio to ensure that it remains aligned with the investor's financial goals, risk tolerance, and investment horizon. This ongoing process involves rebalancing the portfolio to its original asset allocation, which may have shifted due to market movements.

Ultimately, diversification is about creating a balanced portfolio that can withstand the test of time and market fluctuations. It reflects a disciplined approach to investing, where the focus is on long-term growth and stability rather than short-term gains. By understanding and implementing diversification, investors can navigate the complexities of financial markets with greater confidence and resilience.

INVESTMENT STRATEGIES

Navigating the intricate landscape of investment strategies is akin to mastering a complex art form, where knowledge, timing, and the ability to anticipate market trends converge. In the pursuit of wealth creation, investment strategies serve as the essential tools that guide investors in making informed decisions, ultimately determining the trajectory of their financial growth. Understanding the nuances of these strategies is crucial, as they provide the framework for constructing a robust investment portfolio tailored to individual risk appetites and financial goals.

At the heart of successful investing lies the principle of diversification. This strategy involves spreading investments across various asset classes, such as stocks, bonds, real estate, and commodities, to mitigate risk and enhance potential returns. By allocating resources across different sectors and geographic regions, investors can cushion their portfolios against market volatility and unforeseen economic downturns. Diversification acts as a safety net, ensuring that the underperformance of one asset does not drastically impact the overall value of the portfolio.

Another pivotal strategy is value investing, which is rooted in the philosophy of identifying undervalued stocks in the market. This approach involves meticulous analysis of a company's financial statements, management practices, and competitive positioning to determine its intrinsic value. Investors who adopt this strategy seek to purchase stocks at a price lower than their perceived worth, with the expectation that the market will eventually recognize the company's true value, leading to substantial capital appreciation. This long-term approach requires patience and a keen eye for identifying opportunities that others might overlook.

Growth investing, on the other hand, focuses on companies that exhibit significant potential for expansion and revenue growth. This strategy often targets firms in emerging industries or those with innovative products and services. Growth investors are less concerned with current earnings and more focused on the future prospects of a company, betting on its ability to outperform the market over time. While this strategy can yield high returns, it also carries greater risk, as growth stocks can be more volatile and sensitive to market fluctuations.

Income investing emphasizes generating a steady stream of income through dividends or interest payments, appealing to investors seeking regular cash flow. This strategy typically involves investments in dividend-paying stocks, bonds, and real estate investment trusts (REITs). Income investors prioritize stability and consistent returns, often opting for well-established companies with a history of reliable dividend payments. This approach provides a buffer against market volatility, offering a degree of financial security through passive income.

Technical analysis, a strategy employed by traders and investors alike, involves studying historical price movements and trading volumes to forecast future market behavior. By analyzing charts and identifying patterns, technical analysts aim to predict short-term price movements and capitalize on them. This approach requires a deep understanding of market psychology and the ability to interpret complex data, making it a favored strategy among active traders who seek to exploit market inefficiencies.

In the realm of wealth creation, the selection and implementation of investment strategies play a pivotal role in shaping an investor's financial journey. Each strategy offers unique advantages and challenges, requiring a thoughtful consideration of personal objectives, risk tolerance, and market conditions. Mastery of these strategies enables investors to navigate the financial markets with confidence, laying the foundation for enduring wealth and financial prosperity.

6

Chapter 5: Advanced Investment Strategies

OPTIONS AND FUTURES

In the intricate tapestry of financial markets, options and futures emerge as powerful instruments, offering a realm of possibilities for both seasoned investors and novices alike. These derivatives, rooted in the fundamental principles of trading, provide a sophisticated means to hedge risks, speculate on price movements, and enhance portfolio diversification. At their core, options and futures are contracts that derive their value from an underlying asset, which can range from stocks and commodities to currencies and indices. This intrinsic quality allows traders to engage in transactions without necessarily owning the underlying asset, thereby amplifying potential returns while concurrently managing exposure to risk.

Options, in their varied forms, offer the right, but not the obligation, to buy or sell an asset at a predetermined price within a specified time frame. This flexibility is encapsulated in two primary types: call options, which confer the right to purchase, and put options, which grant the right to sell. The strategic use of options can facilitate intricate trading strategies, such as protective puts for safeguarding investments or covered calls for generating additional income. The allure of options lies in their ability to provide leverage, enabling investors to control a large position with a relatively modest capital outlay. However, this leverage also underscores the importance of astute risk management, as the potential for rapid losses is as significant as the opportunity for substantial gains.

Futures contracts, on the other hand, obligate the holder to buy or sell an asset at a future date for a price agreed upon today. These standardized contracts are commonly used in commodities markets, where they serve a dual purpose: enabling producers and consumers to lock in prices and allowing speculators to profit from price fluctuations. The structure of futures markets, characterized by centralized exchanges and uniform contract specifications, enhances liquidity and transparency. This environment fosters a dynamic interplay of market forces, where participants can engage in arbitrage, hedging, or speculative activities. The leverage inherent in futures trading magnifies both potential profits and losses, necessitating a disciplined approach to position management and margin requirements.

The interplay between options and futures extends beyond their individual characteristics, offering a synergistic approach to trading and investment strategies. By combining these instruments, market participants can construct sophisticated portfolios that exploit market inefficiencies, hedge against adverse movements, and optimize returns. For instance, futures can be employed to set a directional bias, while options can provide a protective overlay or capitalize on volatility. This versatility is a testament to the depth and complexity of derivatives markets, where creativity and analytical prowess converge to unlock financial opportunities.

Navigating the realm of options and futures demands a comprehensive understanding of market dynamics, pricing models, and strategic implementation. Mastery in this domain is not merely an academic pursuit but a practical endeavor that requires continuous learning and adaptation. As financial markets evolve, so too do the instruments and strategies that underpin them, challenging traders and investors to refine their skills and expand their horizons. In this ever-changing landscape, options and futures remain indispensable tools for those seeking to harness the potential of the markets and achieve mastery in wealth creation.

CRYPTOCURRENCY

In the ever-evolving landscape of modern finance, a revolutionary concept has emerged, transforming the way individuals perceive and engage with money. Cryptocurrency, a digital or virtual form of currency that utilizes cryptography for security, is reshaping the economic fabric of the world. Unlike traditional currencies issued by governments and central banks, cryptocurrencies operate on decentralized platforms, primarily using blockchain technology, which ensures transparency, security, and immutability of transactions. This innovative approach to currency has captured the imagination of investors, technologists, and visionaries alike, offering a glimpse into a future where financial transactions are not only more secure but also more inclusive.

The allure of cryptocurrency lies in its decentralized nature. Free from the constraints of traditional banking systems and governmental oversight, it provides users with unprecedented control over their financial assets. This autonomy is achieved through blockchain technology, which records every transaction in a distributed ledger that is accessible to all participants in the network. Each block in the chain contains a set of transactions, and once verified, it is timestamped and added to the chain in a chronological order, creating a permanent and unalterable record. This level of transparency reduces the risk of fraud and corruption, making it an attractive option for those seeking an alternative to conventional banking.

Bitcoin, the first and most well-known cryptocurrency, paved the way for this digital revolution. Introduced in 2009 by an anonymous entity known as Satoshi Nakamoto, Bitcoin demonstrated the potential of a peer-to-peer electronic cash system that eliminates the need for intermediaries. Its success has spurred the development of thousands of alternative cryptocurrencies, each with unique features and uses. Ethereum, for example, extends the concept of blockchain by enabling smart contracts—self-executing contracts with the terms of the agreement directly written into code. These innovations are not only transforming the financial sector but also influencing other industries, such as supply chain management, healthcare, and real estate, by enhancing efficiency and reducing costs.

Despite its many advantages, cryptocurrency is not without challenges. The volatility of digital currencies like Bitcoin and Ethereum has been a significant concern for investors. Prices can fluctuate dramatically within short periods, leading to substantial financial gains or losses. Additionally, the regulatory environment surrounding cryptocurrencies is still evolving, with governments worldwide grappling with how to classify and regulate these digital assets. Concerns about security, particularly in the wake of high-profile hacking incidents and fraudulent schemes, have also cast a shadow over the cryptocurrency market, prompting calls for more robust security measures and oversight.

Nevertheless, the potential of cryptocurrency to democratize finance and empower individuals cannot be understated. As more people gain access to the internet and digital technologies, cryptocurrencies offer a viable solution to the unbanked populations in developing regions, providing them with access to financial services that were previously out of reach. This digital currency revolution is not only reshaping the way we think about money but also redefining the very foundations of wealth creation in the 21st century. As we stand on the brink of this new financial frontier, the possibilities seem as limitless as the technology itself.

REAL ESTATE SYNDICATION

In the intricate world of wealth creation, real estate syndication emerges as a sophisticated strategy, offering investors a unique avenue to participate in large-scale property investments. At its core, real estate syndication is a partnership between multiple investors who pool their resources to purchase, manage, and profit from real estate ventures that would otherwise be beyond their individual financial reach. This collaborative investment model not only democratizes access to high-value properties but also diversifies risk and amplifies potential returns.

The process begins with the identification of a promising real estate opportunity, typically by a seasoned syndicator or sponsor. This individual or entity is responsible for the acquisition, management, and eventual sale of the property. The sponsor plays a pivotal role, leveraging their expertise to navigate the complexities of real estate markets, perform due diligence, and secure financing. Their experience and reputation are often key factors in attracting passive investors who rely on the sponsor's capabilities to drive the investment to success.

Once a viable property is identified, the sponsor outlines the investment strategy and financial projections, creating a comprehensive business plan. This document serves as a blueprint for potential investors, detailing the expected timeline, cash flow projections, and exit strategy. Transparency is crucial at this stage, as investors need to understand the risks involved and the potential for returns. The business plan also clarifies the structure of the syndication, including the distribution of profits and the management fees allocated to the sponsor.

Investors, often referred to as limited partners, contribute capital to the syndication, acquiring an ownership stake in the property proportional to their investment. Unlike the sponsor, these investors are typically passive participants, entrusting the day-to-day operations and strategic decisions to the sponsor. This arrangement allows investors to benefit from the income and appreciation of real estate without the responsibilities and challenges of direct property management.

One of the primary advantages of real estate syndication is the ability to invest in properties that offer significant growth potential, such as commercial buildings, apartment complexes, or large residential developments. These assets often require substantial capital and expertise to manage, making them inaccessible to individual investors. By pooling resources, syndications can acquire these high-value properties, enabling investors to diversify their portfolios and access markets they might otherwise be unable to enter.

Additionally, real estate syndication offers tax benefits that can enhance overall returns. The income generated from these investments is often shielded by depreciation and other tax deductions, reducing the taxable income for investors. This aspect is particularly attractive to high-net-worth individuals seeking to optimize their tax liabilities while growing their wealth.

However, like any investment vehicle, real estate syndication carries inherent risks. Market fluctuations, changes in interest rates, and property-specific challenges can impact the profitability of the venture. Therefore, thorough due diligence and a clear understanding of the investment's risk profile are essential for potential investors.

In essence, real estate syndication represents a powerful tool in the arsenal of wealth creation strategies. It combines the strengths of collective investment with the expertise of seasoned professionals, offering investors the opportunity to participate in lucrative real estate markets while mitigating individual risk. As a result, it continues to attract savvy investors seeking to expand their financial horizons and achieve long-term growth.

PRIVATE EQUITY

Private equity represents a unique segment of the financial landscape that offers investors the opportunity to engage in long-term wealth creation through investments in private companies. Unlike public equity, which involves trading shares of publicly listed companies on stock exchanges, private equity focuses on acquiring equity ownership in companies that are not publicly traded. This approach provides investors with the potential for significant returns, albeit with higher risk and longer investment horizons.

The essence of private equity lies in its ability to transform businesses. Private equity firms typically acquire companies with the intention of improving them operationally, strategically, and financially. This often involves a hands-on approach where the private equity firm works closely with the company's management team to implement changes that enhance the company's value. These changes might include restructuring operations, optimizing financial structures, or entering new markets. The ultimate goal is to increase the company's profitability and market value, thereby generating substantial returns upon exit, which could be through a sale or an initial public offering (IPO).

Investors in private equity funds are typically institutional investors, such as pension funds, insurance companies, and endowments, as well as high-net-worth individuals. These investors commit capital to a private equity fund, managed by a private equity firm, which then invests in various private companies. The fund is structured as a limited partnership, where the private equity firm acts as the general partner and the investors are limited partners. The general partner is responsible for making investment decisions and managing the portfolio, while the limited partners provide the capital but have limited involvement in the day-to-day operations.

One of the defining characteristics of private equity is its illiquidity. Unlike publicly traded stocks that can be bought and sold on the stock exchange at any time, private equity investments are typically locked in for a period of 5 to 10 years. This illiquidity is compensated by the potential for higher returns, as private equity investments often aim for returns that exceed those available in public markets. However, this also means that investors must be willing to commit their capital for an extended period and be comfortable with the associated risks.

The private equity market has evolved significantly over the years, becoming a crucial component of the global financial system. It has facilitated the growth and expansion of numerous companies across various industries, driving innovation and economic development. Additionally, private equity has contributed to job creation and technological advancements, making it an influential force in shaping the business landscape.

Despite its potential for high returns, private equity is not without challenges. The success of a private equity investment largely depends on the ability to select the right companies, implement effective strategies, and time the exit correctly. Moreover, the competitive nature of the market means that private equity firms must continuously innovate and adapt to changing economic conditions and regulatory environments.

Understanding the intricacies of private equity is essential for anyone looking to master wealth creation. It requires a deep knowledge of financial analysis, strategic planning, and risk management. For investors willing to navigate its complexities, private equity offers a compelling avenue for achieving substantial long-term gains.

7

Chapter 6: Entrepreneurship and Wealth

STARTING A BUSINESS

The road to wealth creation is often paved with the establishment of a business, a venture where dreams and reality converge. It is a place where visionaries translate their aspirations into tangible entities, filled with potential and promise. The process begins with an idea, a spark of innovation that ignites the entrepreneurial spirit. This idea is the seed from which a thriving business can grow, nurtured by the dedication and passion of its founder.

The initial stages of starting a business require careful planning and consideration. Entrepreneurs must conduct thorough market research to understand the landscape in which they wish to operate. This involves identifying target audiences, analyzing competitors, and recognizing trends that could influence the business's trajectory. Armed with this knowledge, the entrepreneur can craft a business plan, a blueprint that outlines the strategic approach to achieving success. This plan serves as a guiding document, detailing the business model, financial forecasts, marketing strategies, and operational structures.

Securing funding is often the next critical step. Entrepreneurs may turn to various sources, such as personal savings, angel investors, venture capitalists, or crowdfunding platforms. Each option comes with its own set of advantages and challenges, requiring a strategic approach to align with the business's long-term goals. The ability to present a compelling case to potential investors is crucial, showcasing the business's potential for growth and profitability.

As the business takes shape, the legal framework becomes an essential consideration. Entrepreneurs must decide on the appropriate business structure, whether it be a sole proprietorship, partnership, corporation, or limited liability company. Each structure has distinct implications for liability, taxation, and regulatory compliance, influencing the business's operational dynamics. Additionally, securing necessary permits and licenses ensures that the business operates within the legal boundaries set by local and national authorities.

Building a strong brand identity is another pivotal aspect of starting a business. This involves developing a unique value proposition that distinguishes the business from its competitors. A well-crafted brand resonates with customers, fostering trust and loyalty. Entrepreneurs must pay attention to visual elements such as logos and color schemes, as well as the tone and voice of their communications. Consistency across all platforms strengthens the brand's presence in the market.

The recruitment of a dedicated team is integral to the business's success. Entrepreneurs must identify individuals who share their vision and possess the skills necessary to drive the business forward. A cohesive team can navigate challenges effectively, leveraging diverse perspectives to innovate and improve. Establishing a positive company culture from the outset encourages collaboration and motivates employees to contribute to the business's objectives.

In the digital age, an online presence is indispensable. Creating a user-friendly website and engaging with customers on social media platforms expands the business's reach and enhances visibility. Digital marketing strategies, such as search engine optimization and content marketing, attract and retain customers, driving growth and revenue.

Starting a business is a multifaceted endeavor that demands resilience, creativity, and strategic acumen. It is a journey filled with challenges and opportunities, where each decision can shape the trajectory of the venture. With a solid foundation and a clear vision, entrepreneurs can navigate this complex landscape, laying the groundwork for wealth creation and a prosperous future.

SCALING YOUR BUSINESS

Amidst the bustling corridors of enterprise, the concept of scaling a business emerges as a pivotal milestone in the journey toward wealth creation. As a seedling of an idea transforms into a flourishing entity, the necessity to expand becomes an essential step that promises not only growth but also sustainability in an ever-competitive landscape. Scaling a business is akin to orchestrating a symphony where every note, every instrument, and every pause must harmonize to produce a masterpiece.

The foundation of scaling lies in understanding the core competencies of the business. Identifying what sets the business apart from its competitors is crucial. This involves a detailed analysis of the products or services offered, the unique selling propositions, and how these elements can be leveraged to capture a larger market share. A successful scale-up strategy requires a deep dive into the intricacies of the business model, ensuring that it is robust enough to withstand the pressures of expansion.

Infrastructure plays a significant role in the scaling process. It is imperative to evaluate whether the existing systems, technology, and processes can support an increase in demand. This often necessitates an investment in upgrading technology, optimizing processes, and sometimes even restructuring the organization to create more efficient workflows. The goal is to create a scalable infrastructure that can adapt to the dynamic needs of a growing enterprise.

The human element cannot be overlooked when considering scaling. A business is only as strong as its people, and scaling successfully requires a team that is both capable and motivated. This involves strategic hiring practices, investing in employee training, and fostering a company culture that values innovation and adaptability. As the business grows, so too must the skills and capabilities of its workforce.

Market expansion is another critical aspect of scaling a business. This could involve exploring new geographical markets, diversifying the product line, or even targeting a different customer segment. Each of these strategies comes with its own set of challenges and opportunities, requiring careful market research and a well-thought-out marketing strategy. Understanding the nuances of different markets and tailoring offerings to meet the specific needs and preferences of each is a delicate balancing act.

Financial planning is the backbone of any scaling strategy. It requires a thorough assessment of the financial health of the business, ensuring that there is enough capital to support growth initiatives. This might involve securing additional funding through investors or loans, managing cash flow efficiently, and keeping a close eye on profitability margins. Every financial decision should align with the overarching goal of sustainable growth.

Risk management is another crucial component. Scaling a business involves venturing into uncharted territories, which naturally comes with a degree of risk. It is essential to identify potential risks, whether operational, financial, or market-related, and develop strategies to mitigate them. This proactive approach ensures that the business remains resilient in the face of challenges.

In essence, scaling a business is a multifaceted endeavor that requires strategic foresight, meticulous planning, and an unwavering commitment to excellence. It is the art of balancing ambition with practicality, ensuring that growth is not only achieved but sustained over the long term.

INNOVATION AND DISRUPTION

In the rapidly evolving landscape of wealth creation, innovation often serves as both a beacon and a catalyst, guiding individuals and enterprises towards new frontiers. The relentless pace of technological advancement has fundamentally reshaped the way wealth is generated, distributed, and perceived. Innovations, whether in technology, finance, or business models, are the lifeblood of economic growth and prosperity. They drive productivity, open up new markets, and create opportunities for those agile enough to harness their potential.

Consider the transformative impact of digital technology. The advent of the internet and mobile connectivity has democratized access to information and resources, enabling anyone with a device and an idea to potentially reach a global audience. This technological democratization has lowered barriers to entry across industries, allowing entrepreneurs from diverse backgrounds to innovate and compete on an unprecedented scale. The rise of platforms like social media, e-commerce, and fintech exemplifies how digital innovation can disrupt traditional business models, creating new pathways for wealth accumulation.

Disruption, however, is the other side of the innovation coin. While innovation propels progress, it also challenges established norms and practices, often rendering existing skills and business models obsolete. This dynamic creates a complex environment where adaptation is crucial for survival. Companies that fail to innovate or respond to disruptive forces risk losing their competitive edge, as seen in the decline of once-dominant firms that were slow to embrace change.

The financial sector offers a vivid illustration of this phenomenon. Traditional banking institutions, once the gatekeepers of financial transactions, find themselves competing with nimble fintech startups offering faster, more efficient services through innovative technologies like blockchain and artificial intelligence. These technologies not only enhance operational efficiency but also offer greater transparency and security, appealing to a tech-savvy consumer base that demands more from financial services.

Innovation and disruption are not confined to technology alone; they permeate all facets of wealth creation. In real estate, the sharing economy has redefined ownership and investment through platforms like Airbnb, challenging the conventional notions of property utilization and investment returns. Similarly, in the energy sector, renewable technologies are disrupting fossil fuel dominance, paving the way for sustainable wealth creation that aligns with global environmental goals.

The interplay between innovation and disruption underscores the importance of a forward-thinking mindset. Those who thrive in this environment are often characterized by their ability to anticipate trends, embrace uncertainty, and leverage emerging technologies to create value. This requires a willingness to experiment, take calculated risks, and continually adapt to changing circumstances.

The relentless drive for innovation and the inevitability of disruption present both challenges and opportunities. For wealth creators, the key lies in cultivating a culture of innovation that is responsive to change, while also being resilient in the face of disruption. This delicate balance is essential for navigating the complexities of modern wealth creation, ensuring sustained growth and prosperity in an ever-changing world.

EXIT STRATEGIES

Navigating the complex world of investments often requires a keen understanding of when and how to exit a venture. This subchapter delves into the art of crafting effective exit strategies, a crucial component of wealth creation. An exit strategy is not merely about liquidating assets or selling a business; it is a meticulously planned process that ensures the maximization of returns and the achievement of financial goals. It encompasses a range of considerations, from market conditions to personal financial objectives.

At the heart of a successful exit strategy is the anticipation of market trends and the ability to adapt to changes. Investors must remain vigilant, continuously assessing the economic environment to identify the optimal moment to exit. This requires a blend of intuition and analytical prowess, as market dynamics can shift rapidly, influenced by factors such as technological advancements, regulatory changes, and geopolitical events.

Moreover, personal objectives play a significant role in shaping an exit strategy. Whether the goal is to retire comfortably, reinvest in new ventures, or simply enjoy the fruits of one's labor, clarity of purpose guides the decision-making process. For some, the allure of a strategic acquisition by a larger entity may present the perfect opportunity, while others may opt for a gradual divestment, allowing for a steady income stream over time.

A well-defined exit strategy also considers the potential tax implications and legal intricacies associated with divestment. Engaging with financial advisors and legal experts can provide valuable insights, helping to navigate the complexities of capital gains taxes, estate planning, and regulatory compliance. This proactive approach ensures that the transition is smooth and financially beneficial.

In addition to these practical considerations, emotional readiness is an often-overlooked aspect of exiting an investment. The attachment to a business or asset can cloud judgment, making it challenging to make objective decisions. Investors must cultivate a mindset that views exit strategies as a natural progression in the wealth creation journey, rather than an end.

Diversification remains a cornerstone of risk management in exit planning. By spreading investments across various asset classes and industries, investors mitigate the impact of market volatility on their portfolios. This approach not only enhances the potential for returns but also provides multiple exit avenues, reducing reliance on a single investment.

Ultimately, the development of a robust exit strategy is a

dynamic process, requiring continuous evaluation and adjustment. It demands a comprehensive understanding of both the financial landscape and personal aspirations. By integrating these elements, investors can craft strategies that not only safeguard their wealth but also propel them toward future financial success. The essence of a successful exit lies in its ability to seamlessly transition an investor from one phase of wealth creation to the next, ensuring that the journey is as rewarding as the destination itself.

8

Chapter 7: The Role of Technology in Wealth Creation

FINTECH INNOVATIONS

Within the ever-evolving landscape of financial technology, an array of innovations has emerged, fundamentally transforming the way individuals and institutions manage wealth. These fintech advancements are characterized by their ability to streamline financial processes, enhance accessibility, and provide unprecedented opportunities for wealth creation. At the heart of these innovations lies a synergy between advanced technology and financial acumen, resulting in tools and platforms that cater to the diverse needs of modern investors and consumers.

One of the most significant developments in this arena is the rise of digital payment systems. These systems have revolutionized traditional transaction methods, offering seamless, secure, and instantaneous payment solutions. By leveraging cutting-edge technology, such as blockchain and artificial intelligence, digital payment platforms facilitate transactions across borders with minimal fees and reduced processing times. This not only enhances convenience for consumers but also opens up new avenues for businesses to expand their reach globally.

Robo-advisors represent another groundbreaking innovation within the fintech domain. These automated platforms harness the power of algorithms to provide personalized investment advice and portfolio management services. By analyzing vast amounts of data, robo-advisors offer tailored investment strategies that align with individual risk profiles and financial goals. This democratization of investment management makes sophisticated financial planning accessible to a broader audience, empowering individuals who may have previously found traditional advisory services cost-prohibitive.

Peer-to-peer lending platforms are also reshaping the financial landscape by connecting borrowers directly with lenders, bypassing traditional banking intermediaries. These platforms utilize technology to assess creditworthiness and facilitate transactions, offering competitive interest rates and flexible terms. For investors, peer-to-peer lending provides an alternative investment opportunity with the potential for attractive returns, while borrowers benefit from increased access to funding.

Moreover, the integration of artificial intelligence and machine learning into financial services has ushered in a new era of personalized banking experiences. AI-driven chatbots and virtual assistants provide real-time customer support, while predictive analytics help financial institutions anticipate customer needs and offer tailored solutions. This personalization enhances customer satisfaction and loyalty, while also improving operational efficiency for financial service providers.

Blockchain technology, with its decentralized and secure nature, has also made a profound impact on the financial sector. Beyond its application in cryptocurrencies, blockchain is being utilized for smart contracts, supply chain finance, and identity verification. These applications promise to increase transparency, reduce fraud, and streamline complex financial processes, ultimately contributing to more efficient wealth management.

The landscape of fintech innovations is continually evolving, driven by a relentless pursuit of efficiency, accessibility, and customer-centric solutions. As these technologies mature, they hold the potential to redefine wealth creation, offering both individuals and enterprises novel ways to achieve financial success. By embracing these innovations, stakeholders in the financial ecosystem can harness the power of technology to navigate the complexities of the modern financial world and unlock new opportunities for growth and prosperity.

AUTOMATION AND AI

In the ever-evolving landscape of wealth creation, the integration of Automation and Artificial Intelligence (AI) has emerged as a transformative force. These technologies are reshaping how individuals and businesses approach financial growth, offering unprecedented opportunities for efficiency and innovation. Automation, in its essence, refers to the use of technology to perform tasks with minimal human intervention. In the realm of finance, this manifests in various forms, from algorithmic trading systems to automated financial planning tools. These systems can analyze vast amounts of data at lightning speed, identifying patterns and trends that might elude human analysts. By automating routine tasks, individuals and businesses can focus on strategic decision-making, ultimately leading to more informed and timely investment choices.

Artificial Intelligence, on the other hand, brings a layer of cognitive capability to automation. AI systems are not just executing tasks; they are learning from data, adapting to new information, and improving their performance over time. In wealth creation, AI is being utilized to develop predictive models that can forecast market movements, assess risk, and optimize asset allocation. These models leverage machine learning algorithms, which enable them to refine their predictions as they process more data. This dynamic learning process allows for a more nuanced understanding of market behaviors, potentially leading to more profitable investment strategies.

The synergy between Automation and AI is particularly evident in the field of robo-advisory services. These platforms use AI-driven algorithms to provide personalized investment advice, tailored to an individual's financial goals and risk tolerance. By automating the advisory process, these services make wealth management accessible to a broader audience, often at a fraction of the cost of traditional financial advisors. This democratization of financial advice is empowering more people to take control of their financial futures, contributing to a more inclusive wealth creation landscape.

Moreover, the implementation of Automation and AI in financial processes extends beyond investment strategies. These technologies are also enhancing operational efficiency within financial institutions. For instance, AI-powered chatbots are revolutionizing customer service by providing instant responses to inquiries, while automated fraud detection systems are improving security by identifying suspicious activities in real-time. These advancements not only reduce operational costs but also enhance the overall customer experience, fostering trust and loyalty in financial services.

Despite the numerous benefits, the integration of Automation and AI in wealth creation is not without challenges. Concerns about data privacy and the ethical implications of AI decision-making are growing. As these technologies become more pervasive, there is a need for robust regulatory frameworks to ensure they are used responsibly and transparently. Additionally, the reliance on automated systems raises questions about the potential loss of human expertise and the risk of over-dependence on technology-driven solutions.

As Automation and AI continue to evolve, their impact on wealth creation will undoubtedly deepen. These technologies are not just tools; they are catalysts for change, driving innovation and redefining the possibilities of financial success. By harnessing their potential, individuals and businesses can navigate the complexities of the modern financial landscape with increased agility and insight.

ONLINE BUSINESS MODELS

In the digital age, the landscape of business has been dramatically transformed by the advent of the internet, leading to the emergence of a variety of online business models that have redefined the way entrepreneurs create wealth. These models offer unprecedented opportunities for scalability, reach, and efficiency, enabling businesses to operate beyond the constraints of traditional brick-and-mortar establishments. Each model presents unique characteristics, advantages, and challenges, catering to different entrepreneurial goals and market needs.

E-commerce has become a cornerstone of online business models, facilitating the buying and selling of goods and services over the internet. Platforms like Amazon, eBay, and Shopify have revolutionized retail, offering businesses access to global markets and consumers the convenience of shopping from anywhere at any time. The success of e-commerce relies heavily on effective digital marketing strategies, customer service, and logistics management to ensure seamless transactions and delivery.

Subscription-based models have gained significant traction, offering consumers ongoing access to products or services in exchange for a recurring fee. This model fosters customer loyalty and provides businesses with a predictable revenue stream. Companies like Netflix, Spotify, and various SaaS providers exemplify the success of this approach, continuously innovating their offerings to retain and grow their subscriber base.

Affiliate marketing is another powerful online business model, where individuals or companies earn commissions by promoting other businesses' products or services. This model benefits from the vast reach of social media and content platforms, allowing affiliates to leverage their audience to drive sales for partner brands. Successful affiliate marketers often build trust and authority in their niche, providing valuable content that naturally incorporates affiliate links.

The gig economy has also flourished online, with platforms like Fiverr, Upwork, and TaskRabbit connecting freelancers with clients seeking specific skills or services. This model provides flexibility for both workers and employers, enabling businesses to tap into a global talent pool while allowing individuals to monetize their skills on their own terms. The rise of remote work has further accelerated the adoption of this model, making it an integral part of the modern business ecosystem.

Digital products, such as e-books, online courses, and software, represent another lucrative online business model. These products can be created once and sold repeatedly with minimal additional cost, offering high profit margins. Entrepreneurs in this space often focus on niche markets, leveraging their expertise to provide valuable insights or tools that cater to specific audiences. Platforms like Udemy and Gumroad have made it easier for creators to distribute and monetize their digital products.

Crowdfunding has emerged as a viable model for entrepreneurs seeking to raise capital online. Websites like Kickstarter and Indiegogo allow creators to pitch their projects directly to potential backers, democratizing the funding process. This model not only provides financial support but also validates business ideas and builds an initial customer base. Successful crowdfunding campaigns often rely on compelling storytelling and strategic marketing to capture the attention and support of potential investors.

Each of these online business models offers distinct pathways to wealth creation, requiring entrepreneurs to carefully consider their strengths, resources, and target markets. The dynamic nature of the internet ensures that these models continue to evolve, presenting new opportunities and challenges for those willing to navigate the digital frontier.

DIGITAL MARKETING

In the rapidly evolving landscape of wealth creation, digital marketing emerges as a pivotal tool, bridging the gap between businesses and their audiences in the digital age. It encompasses a broad spectrum of strategies and practices designed to promote products and services through digital channels, engaging consumers in a more interactive and measurable way than traditional marketing methods. The essence of digital marketing lies in its ability to leverage the internet and other digital platforms to reach a global audience, thus democratizing marketing efforts for businesses of all sizes.

At its core, digital marketing is characterized by several key components, each playing a unique role in the overall strategy. Search Engine Optimization (SEO) is foundational, focusing on enhancing a website's visibility on search engines like Google.

By optimizing content and utilizing relevant keywords, businesses can attract organic traffic, ensuring that their offerings are accessible to potential customers actively seeking related products or services. This organic reach is complemented by Search Engine Marketing (SEM), which involves paid advertising efforts to further boost visibility and drive targeted traffic to a website.

Social media marketing is another critical aspect, harnessing platforms such as Facebook, Instagram, Twitter, and LinkedIn to connect with consumers. These platforms offer businesses the opportunity to engage with their audience in a more personal and interactive manner, fostering brand loyalty and community building. Through creative content and targeted advertising, companies can reach specific demographics, tailoring their messages to resonate with different segments of their audience.

Email marketing continues to be a powerful tool within the digital marketing arsenal. By sending personalized and targeted messages directly to consumers' inboxes, businesses can nurture leads, maintain customer relationships, and drive conversions. The effectiveness of email marketing lies in its ability to deliver relevant content to a receptive audience, providing value and encouraging engagement.

Content marketing plays a crucial role in establishing authority and building trust with consumers. By creating informative, engaging, and valuable content, businesses can position themselves as industry leaders and thought influencers. This approach not only attracts potential customers but also retains them by consistently providing insights and solutions to their needs and challenges.

The analytical nature of digital marketing allows for meticulous tracking and measurement of campaign performance. Through tools like Google Analytics and social media insights, businesses can gain valuable data on consumer behavior, campaign effectiveness, and return on investment. This data-driven approach enables marketers to refine their strategies, optimize their efforts, and make informed decisions, ensuring that resources are allocated efficiently.

In the realm of wealth creation, digital marketing serves as a catalyst for growth, enabling businesses to expand their reach, enhance brand awareness, and ultimately drive revenue. As technology continues to advance, the landscape of digital marketing will evolve, presenting new opportunities and challenges for those seeking to master the art of wealth creation through digital channels. Embracing these tools and strategies is essential for any modern entrepreneur or business aiming to thrive in today's competitive market.

9

Chapter 8: Tax Planning and Wealth

UNDERSTANDING TAXES

Taxes are an integral aspect of financial planning and wealth management, playing a pivotal role in shaping one's financial future. Recognizing the intricacies of the tax system is essential for anyone aiming to master wealth creation. Taxes are imposed by governments to fund public services and infrastructure, and they come in various forms, including income tax, sales tax, property tax, and capital gains tax, among others. Each type of tax has its own set of rules and rates, which can vary significantly depending on the jurisdiction and the individual's financial situation.

The concept of taxation is rooted in the principle of contributing to the common good. However, the complexity of tax codes can often be overwhelming, making it crucial for individuals to develop a solid understanding of how taxes affect their financial decisions. By doing so, they can devise strategies to minimize their tax liabilities legally, thereby maximizing their wealth accumulation potential.

Income tax is arguably the most familiar form of taxation, as it directly impacts the earnings of individuals and businesses. It is typically calculated based on a progressive tax system, where higher income levels are taxed at higher rates. This system is designed to ensure that those with greater financial resources contribute a larger share to the funding of public services. Understanding the nuances of income tax brackets, deductions, and credits is vital for effective tax planning.

Capital gains tax is another significant consideration, particularly for investors and those involved in buying and selling assets. This tax is levied on the profit made from the sale of assets such as stocks, bonds, or real estate. The rate at which capital gains are taxed can differ based on how long the asset was held before being sold, distinguishing between short-term and long-term capital gains. Long-term capital gains often enjoy more favorable tax rates, incentivizing investors to hold onto their assets for extended periods.

Property taxes are imposed on real estate ownership and are usually based on the assessed value of the property. These taxes fund local services such as schools, roads, and emergency services. Understanding how property taxes are calculated and the exemptions available can significantly impact the overall cost of owning real estate.

Sales tax is a consumption tax imposed on the sale of goods and services. It is typically a percentage of the purchase price and is collected at the point of sale. While sales tax may seem straightforward, the rates can vary widely depending on the location and type of goods or services purchased.

Navigating the world of taxes requires a proactive approach and a willingness to stay informed about changes in tax laws and regulations. Engaging with tax professionals or utilizing tax software can provide valuable insights and assistance in managing tax obligations effectively. Ultimately, understanding taxes is not just about compliance but about leveraging this knowledge to make informed financial decisions that support long-term wealth creation. By mastering the art of tax planning, individuals can ensure that they retain more of their hard-earned money, paving the way for a more secure and prosperous financial future.

TAX-EFFICIENT INVESTMENTS

Navigating the intricate world of investments can often seem like a daunting task, particularly when considering the implications of taxes. However, understanding and implementing tax-efficient investment strategies is crucial for maximizing returns and preserving wealth. Tax-efficient investments are those that are structured to minimize tax liabilities and enhance after-tax returns, allowing investors to keep more of their earnings.

One of the key elements of tax-efficient investing is asset location. This involves strategically placing different types of investments in accounts that offer the most favorable tax treatment. For instance, placing tax-inefficient assets in tax-deferred accounts such as traditional IRAs or 401(k)s can defer taxes until withdrawal, potentially lowering the overall tax burden. Conversely, tax-efficient assets like municipal bonds, which are often exempt from federal taxes, can be held in taxable accounts to take advantage of their favorable tax status.

Another important aspect is the selection of tax-efficient investment vehicles. Index funds and exchange-traded funds (ETFs) are typically more tax-efficient compared to actively managed funds. This is because they generally have lower turnover rates, resulting in fewer taxable capital gains distributions. Additionally, capital gains from these funds are often long-term, which are taxed at a lower rate than short-term gains, further contributing to tax efficiency.

Investors can also benefit from tax-loss harvesting, a strategy that involves selling investments at a loss to offset capital gains tax liabilities. By strategically realizing losses, investors can reduce their taxable income and potentially improve their overall tax situation. This technique requires careful timing and consideration of market conditions, but when executed correctly, it can significantly enhance after-tax returns.

Diversification also plays a role in tax-efficient investing. A well-diversified portfolio can help manage risk and provide opportunities to optimize tax outcomes. For example, holding a mix of investments across various asset classes can allow investors to take advantage of different tax treatments and timing strategies. Furthermore, diversification can help mitigate the impact of any single investment's poor performance on the overall portfolio, thereby preserving wealth.

Tax-efficient investments are not solely about minimizing taxes today but also about strategic planning for the future. Long-term investment strategies often focus on compounding returns while managing tax liabilities over time. This involves making informed decisions about when to realize gains, how to allocate assets, and which accounts to utilize for specific investments.

Furthermore, staying informed about changes in tax laws and regulations is essential for maintaining a tax-efficient investment strategy. Tax policies can change, and staying proactive in understanding these changes can help investors adapt their strategies accordingly. Consulting with tax professionals or financial advisors can provide valuable insights and guidance tailored to individual circumstances.

Incorporating tax-efficient strategies into an investment plan requires diligence and a keen understanding of both the financial markets and tax landscape. By prioritizing tax efficiency, investors can enhance their potential for wealth accumulation and retention, ensuring that more of their hard-earned money remains in their own hands to support their financial goals and aspirations.

RETIREMENT ACCOUNTS

In the intricate landscape of financial planning, retirement accounts stand as pivotal instruments for securing a stable future. These accounts, designed specifically to support individuals in their post-career years, are integral components of a comprehensive wealth creation strategy. Understanding the nuances of different retirement accounts is crucial for maximizing their potential benefits.

Retirement accounts come in various forms, each with unique characteristics, tax implications, and contribution limits. Among the most common are the Individual Retirement Account (IRA), the 401(k), and the Roth IRA. Each of these accounts offers distinct advantages, and choosing the right one depends on an individual's financial goals, employment situation, and tax considerations.

An IRA, or Individual Retirement Account, provides a flexible option for individuals to contribute towards their retirement independently of their employer. Contributions to a traditional IRA may be tax-deductible, depending on the individual's income and participation in an employer-sponsored plan. The earnings within the account grow tax-deferred, meaning taxes are not paid until withdrawals are made during retirement. This tax deferral can be a powerful tool for compounding growth over time.

In contrast, a Roth IRA offers tax-free growth and tax-free withdrawals in retirement, provided certain conditions are met. Contributions to a Roth IRA are made with after-tax dollars, eliminating the immediate tax benefit but offering significant tax advantages in the future. This can be particularly beneficial for individuals who anticipate being in a higher tax bracket during retirement or who value the security of tax-free income later in life.

Employer-sponsored plans, such as the 401(k), are another cornerstone of retirement planning. These plans allow employees to contribute a portion of their salary to a retirement account, often with pre-tax dollars, reducing their taxable income. Many employers offer matching contributions, effectively providing free money to employees who participate in the plan. This match can significantly enhance the growth potential of the retirement savings.

Understanding the rules regarding contributions and withdrawals is vital. Contribution limits for IRAs and 401(k)s are subject to annual adjustments by the IRS, reflecting inflation and changing economic conditions. Additionally, early withdrawals from these accounts may incur penalties and taxes, emphasizing the importance of these funds being earmarked strictly for retirement.

Diversification within retirement accounts is another critical factor. Allocating investments across a range of asset classes, such as stocks, bonds, and mutual funds, can mitigate risk and optimize returns. Many retirement accounts offer a variety of investment options, allowing account holders to tailor their portfolios to match their risk tolerance and retirement timeline.

Navigating the complexities of retirement accounts requires careful planning and ongoing evaluation. Regularly reviewing account performance, adjusting contributions, and staying informed about changes in tax laws and retirement regulations are essential practices. By leveraging the strategic advantages of retirement accounts, individuals can lay a solid foundation for financial independence and security in their golden years.

ESTATE PLANNING

When contemplating the intricate tapestry of wealth creation, the threads of estate planning are foundational, binding together the legacy one intends to leave behind. Estate planning is not merely a legal exercise; it is an opportunity to articulate one's values, ensuring that the fruits of labor are preserved and passed on to future generations with clarity and purpose. This process extends beyond the distribution of assets and encompasses a holistic approach to managing affairs, both during one's lifetime and after.

A comprehensive estate plan begins with the drafting of a will, a document that serves as the cornerstone of this endeavor. The will delineates how assets are to be allocated, serving as a guide to prevent disputes among heirs and ensuring that one's wishes are respected. In addition to a will, trusts can be established to manage and protect assets, offering flexibility and control over the timing and conditions of distribution. Trusts are particularly beneficial in minimizing estate taxes and safeguarding wealth from potential creditors or legal challenges.

Beyond these financial instruments, estate planning also involves the designation of powers of attorney. These legal appointments empower trusted individuals to make decisions on one's behalf in the event of incapacitation, covering both financial and healthcare matters. Such provisions ensure that one's affairs are managed according to personal preferences, even when direct oversight is not possible.

Tax considerations are another pivotal aspect of estate planning.

By understanding and leveraging tax laws, individuals can optimize the transfer of wealth, reducing the tax burden on beneficiaries. Strategies such as gifting, charitable donations, and life insurance policies are often employed to enhance the efficiency of wealth transfer, preserving the estate's value for the intended heirs.

Furthermore, estate planning provides a framework for addressing potential family dynamics and complexities. By clearly outlining intentions and expectations, individuals can mitigate misunderstandings and foster harmonious relationships among beneficiaries. This proactive approach not only protects the estate but also honors the legacy of the individual, reflecting their wishes and values.

In the broader context of wealth creation, estate planning is an essential component that ensures the sustainability and longevity of one's financial achievements. It is a dynamic process, requiring regular review and adjustment to accommodate changes in personal circumstances, financial landscapes, and legal frameworks. By engaging in thoughtful estate planning, individuals can craft a legacy that extends beyond monetary wealth, encompassing the ideals and principles they hold dear.

Ultimately, estate planning is an expression of stewardship, a commitment to manage resources wisely and responsibly. It is a testament to foresight and care, allowing individuals to shape their legacy with intention and precision. As the final chapter in the journey of wealth creation, estate planning offers peace of mind, knowing that one's life work will continue to benefit those they cherish, long into the future.

10

Chapter 9: Wealth Preservation

ASSET PROTECTION

In the realm of wealth creation, safeguarding one's assets stands as a pivotal pillar, ensuring the fruits of one's labor remain protected against unforeseen adversities. The intricate dance between risk and security unfolds as individuals seek to shield their wealth from potential threats, ranging from economic downturns to personal liabilities. Asset protection emerges as an essential strategy, woven into the fabric of financial planning, offering a fortress of security that enables wealth to endure and flourish.

The landscape of asset protection is vast and varied, encompassing a multitude of tactics tailored to defend against the myriad risks that can erode financial stability. At the heart of this endeavor lies the understanding that wealth, once accumulated, must be meticulously preserved. This involves a comprehensive approach that not only anticipates potential threats but also implements robust measures to mitigate them. From legal structures that safeguard assets against creditors to insurance policies that provide a safety net against unforeseen events, the arsenal of asset protection tools is diverse and potent.

One of the foundational elements of asset protection is the strategic use of legal entities such as trusts, limited liability companies (LLCs), and corporations. These structures serve as formidable barriers, shielding personal assets from business liabilities and potential lawsuits. By delineating personal and business finances, individuals can effectively compartmentalize risk, ensuring that personal wealth remains insulated from the vicissitudes of the business world.

Moreover, insurance plays a crucial role in the realm of asset protection, offering a reliable defense against the unexpected. From comprehensive property insurance that safeguards physical assets to liability insurance that protects against personal or professional claims, the spectrum of coverage is extensive. Each policy is meticulously crafted to address specific vulnerabilities, providing peace of mind and financial security.

In addition to these structural and insurance-based strategies, asset protection also involves the careful management of debt and liabilities. By maintaining a prudent debt-to-equity ratio and ensuring that liabilities are aligned with one's risk tolerance, individuals can minimize their exposure to financial peril. The judicious use of leverage, coupled with a keen awareness of one's financial landscape, empowers individuals to navigate the complexities of wealth preservation with confidence.

Furthermore, the importance of estate planning cannot be overstated in the context of asset protection. By crafting a well-thought-out estate plan, individuals can ensure that their wealth is transferred efficiently and according to their wishes, minimizing the impact of taxes and legal challenges. Trusts, wills, and other estate planning tools serve as vital components in the overarching strategy of asset protection, enabling the seamless transition of wealth across generations.

Ultimately, the art of asset protection is a dynamic and ongoing process, requiring vigilance and adaptability. As the financial landscape evolves, so too must the strategies employed to safeguard wealth. By remaining informed and proactive, individuals can fortify their financial fortress, ensuring that their assets remain secure and their legacy endures. The journey of wealth creation is thus complemented by the steadfast commitment to asset protection, a testament to the foresight and diligence required to master the complexities of financial prosperity.

INSURANCE STRATEGIES

In the realm of wealth creation, insurance strategies stand as a pivotal pillar, safeguarding assets and ensuring financial stability. This subchapter delves into the nuanced world of insurance, exploring the various strategies that can be employed to protect and enhance one's financial portfolio. Insurance, often perceived merely as a protective measure, is, in fact, a multifaceted tool that can be leveraged for wealth creation.

The foundation of any robust insurance strategy lies in understanding the different types of insurance available and their specific roles in a financial plan. Life insurance, health insurance, property insurance, and liability insurance each serve distinct purposes. Life insurance, for instance, is not only a means of providing for dependents in the event of untimely demise but also functions as a vehicle for investment and tax planning through policies like whole life or universal life insurance. These policies accumulate cash value over time, which can be accessed or borrowed against, offering liquidity and financial flexibility.

Health insurance, on the other hand, is crucial in shielding individuals from the financial devastation that can accompany medical emergencies and chronic illnesses. With the rising costs of healthcare, having a comprehensive health insurance policy is a strategic move to preserve wealth. It ensures that medical expenses do not erode savings or investments, allowing individuals to maintain their financial trajectory.

Property insurance, including homeowners and renters insurance, protects tangible assets from unforeseen events such as natural disasters, theft, or vandalism. By securing one's home and possessions, property insurance prevents significant financial setbacks, allowing individuals to focus on growing their wealth rather than recovering from losses.

Liability insurance is another critical component, safeguarding individuals and businesses from potential lawsuits and claims. As wealth grows, so does the risk of being targeted for legal action. Liability insurance, including umbrella policies, provides an extra layer of protection, ensuring that personal or business assets are not jeopardized by legal proceedings.

Beyond the basic categories, advanced insurance strategies involve maximizing the benefits of these policies. For example, utilizing life insurance for estate planning can help mitigate estate taxes, ensuring that more wealth is passed on to heirs. Business owners can employ key person insurance to protect against the loss of crucial personnel, thereby securing the continuity and stability of their enterprise.

Moreover, the strategic use of annuities can provide a steady stream of income during retirement, complementing other retirement savings and ensuring a stable financial future. Annuities can be tailored to individual needs, offering options for lifetime income or fixed periods, thus aligning with long-term wealth management goals.

In crafting an insurance strategy, it is imperative to conduct a thorough assessment of one's financial situation, risk tolerance, and long-term objectives. Consulting with financial advisors and insurance professionals can provide valuable insights and help tailor policies to fit individual needs. Regularly reviewing and updating insurance coverage ensures that it remains aligned with changing circumstances and evolving financial goals.

Ultimately, effective insurance strategies are about more than just protection; they are about proactively managing risk and leveraging insurance as a tool for wealth creation. By integrating insurance into a comprehensive financial plan, individuals can fortify their financial foundation and pave the way for sustainable wealth growth.

INFLATION AND DEFLATION

In the realm of financial landscapes, the phenomena of inflation and deflation stand as pivotal forces, shaping the very fabric of economic stability and growth. These two contrasting elements, akin to the ebb and flow of tides, influence purchasing power, investment strategies, and overall economic health. Inflation, characterized by a general increase in prices and a corresponding decrease in the purchasing value of money, often emerges in a thriving economy where demand outpaces supply. This upward pressure on prices can be attributed to various factors, including increased consumer spending, rising production costs, and expansive monetary policies. As prices rise, the purchasing power of currency diminishes, eroding savings and impacting fixed-income earners disproportionately. However, moderate inflation is often considered a sign of a growing economy, encouraging spending and investment as consumers and businesses anticipate higher future costs.

Conversely, deflation presents a starkly different picture, marked by a decrease in the general price level of goods and services. This decline in prices can lead to increased purchasing power, yet it often signals underlying economic distress. Deflation can occur during periods of economic contraction, where reduced demand leads to excess supply, prompting businesses to lower prices to stimulate sales. While lower prices might seem beneficial to consumers, prolonged deflation can have detrimental effects on the economy. It can lead to decreased revenues for businesses, resulting in layoffs, reduced wages, and a vicious cycle of reduced spending and further price drops. Moreover, deflation increases the real value of debt, placing additional burdens on borrowers and potentially leading to higher default rates.

The interplay between inflation and deflation requires careful navigation by policymakers and investors alike. Central banks often play a crucial role in managing these forces, utilizing monetary policy tools such as interest rate adjustments and open market operations to maintain price stability. By controlling the money supply and influencing borrowing costs, central banks aim to keep inflation within a target range, fostering an environment conducive to sustainable economic growth. For investors, understanding the implications of inflation and deflation is paramount in crafting resilient portfolios. Inflationary environments might warrant investments in assets that preserve or appreciate in value, such as real estate, commodities, or inflation-protected securities. In contrast, deflationary periods may call for a focus on high-quality bonds and cash reserves, which can gain purchasing power as prices decline.

Ultimately, the dance between inflation and deflation underscores the complexity of economic cycles and their impact on wealth creation. Recognizing the signs and understanding the potential consequences of these forces empowers individuals to make informed decisions, safeguarding their financial well-being amidst the ever-changing economic landscape. In this intricate balance, mastering the art of wealth creation involves not only seizing opportunities but also mitigating risks, ensuring that one's financial journey remains on course regardless of economic fluctuations.

LEGACY PLANNING

In the intricate tapestry of wealth creation, the concept of legacy planning emerges as a pivotal thread, weaving together the past, present, and future. This chapter delves into the profound significance of legacy planning as a crucial element of financial mastery. Legacy planning transcends mere financial allocation; it involves the thoughtful consideration of how one's accumulated wealth will impact future generations, communities, and causes dear to one's heart. It is the art of ensuring that the values and principles that guided one's financial journey continue to resonate and influence after one's lifetime.

At the heart of legacy planning lies a deep understanding of personal values and the legacy one wishes to leave behind. It requires introspection and clarity about what truly matters, beyond the mere accumulation of wealth. This process often begins with defining core values and identifying key priorities, such as family well-being, philanthropic endeavors, or the perpetuation of business interests. By aligning financial strategies with these values, individuals can craft a legacy that reflects their true essence, creating a lasting impact.

The tools and strategies employed in legacy planning are diverse, encompassing wills, trusts, charitable foundations, and more. Each instrument serves a unique purpose, offering flexibility and control over how assets are distributed and utilized. Wills, for instance, provide a straightforward mechanism for asset distribution, while trusts offer greater control, privacy, and potential tax advantages. Charitable foundations enable individuals to support causes they are passionate about, fostering a culture of giving that can inspire future generations.

Moreover, legacy planning is not solely about financial distribution; it involves imparting wisdom, values, and life lessons. This often takes the form of family meetings or written statements that articulate the vision and principles that have guided one's life. Such communications ensure that heirs not only inherit wealth but also understand the responsibilities and opportunities that come with it. By fostering open dialogue and education, individuals can prepare their successors to manage and grow the legacy they leave behind.

Tax considerations play a crucial role in legacy planning, with careful structuring needed to minimize tax liabilities and maximize the transfer of wealth. Estate taxes, gift taxes, and capital gains taxes can significantly impact the value of an inheritance. Strategic planning, such as utilizing exemptions, credits, and timing of gifts, can mitigate these effects, ensuring that more wealth is preserved for future generations.

Another critical aspect of legacy planning is adaptability. As life circumstances and laws evolve, so too must legacy plans. Regular reviews and updates are essential to ensure that the plan remains aligned with current goals and legal frameworks. Flexibility in planning allows individuals to respond to changes, whether they are personal, economic, or legislative, maintaining the integrity and effectiveness of the legacy.

In essence, legacy planning is a testament to the foresight and altruism of individuals who seek to make a meaningful impact beyond their own lifetimes. It is a deliberate and thoughtful process that requires careful consideration, planning, and execution. By engaging in legacy planning, individuals can ensure that their wealth serves a purpose greater than themselves, creating a ripple effect of positive change that endures through the generations.

11

Chapter 10: The Psychology of Wealth

OVERCOMING LIMITING BELIEFS

In the grand tapestry of wealth creation, the threads of belief often weave patterns that can either propel us forward or hold us back. These beliefs, deeply embedded within the psyche, act as unseen forces, influencing our decisions, actions, and ultimately, our financial destiny. Among these beliefs, some serve as powerful allies, fostering growth and abundance, while others, known as limiting beliefs, act as formidable barriers, hindering our progress and potential.

Limiting beliefs are like invisible shackles that bind us to a reality far removed from our true potential. They are often birthed from past experiences, societal conditioning, or inherited narratives, whispering insidious notions of inadequacy, fear, and scarcity. These beliefs might manifest as thoughts such as "I'm not good with money," "Wealth is only for the lucky few," or "I don't deserve financial success." Each of these thoughts, though seemingly innocuous, has the power to dictate the trajectory of our financial journey, keeping us anchored in a cycle of limitation and lack.

To overcome these limiting beliefs, one must first bring them into the light of awareness. This process begins with introspection, a candid examination of the thoughts and assumptions that govern our financial behavior. It requires a willingness to question the narratives we have long accepted as truth, to challenge the very foundation upon which our financial identity is built. This journey of self-discovery is not always comfortable, for it demands confronting deeply held fears and insecurities. However, it is a necessary step towards liberation and empowerment.

Once these limiting beliefs are identified, the next step is to dismantle them. This involves replacing negative narratives with empowering ones, transforming "I can't" into "I can," and "I don't deserve" into "I am worthy." This cognitive restructuring is akin to reprogramming the mind, creating new neural pathways that support a mindset of abundance and possibility. Affirmations, visualization, and positive self-talk are powerful tools in this transformative process, helping to reinforce new beliefs and gradually erode the old.

Moreover, surrounding oneself with positive influences can accelerate this transformation. Engaging with mentors, coaches, or supportive communities that embody the mindset we aspire to adopt can provide encouragement, accountability, and inspiration. These influences serve as a mirror, reflecting back the potential and possibilities we may not yet see within ourselves.

Ultimately, overcoming limiting beliefs is an ongoing process, a continual journey of growth and self-improvement. It requires patience, persistence, and a commitment to personal development. As these beliefs are gradually dismantled, the path to wealth creation becomes clearer, unencumbered by the chains of doubt and fear. In this newfound freedom, the horizon of possibility expands, revealing opportunities for financial abundance that were once hidden from view. With each step forward, the mastery of wealth creation becomes not just a distant dream, but a tangible reality, accessible to all who dare to believe in their own potential.

THE ROLE OF DISCIPLINE

Discipline is the invisible thread that weaves through the tapestry of wealth creation, binding together the diverse elements necessary for financial success. It is the steadfast hand that guides decisions, the unwavering resolve that fuels persistence, and the silent force that transforms dreams into reality. In the pursuit of wealth, discipline manifests as a meticulous adherence to strategies, a commitment to long-term goals, and a resistance to the seductive allure of short-term gratification.

At its core, discipline in wealth creation is about consistency. It requires the establishment and maintenance of habits that support financial growth. This includes regular saving, prudent investing, and continuous education about financial markets and opportunities. Such habits form the bedrock of a disciplined approach, enabling individuals to navigate the complexities of financial landscapes with confidence and foresight.

Discipline also involves a profound understanding of the value of time. It is the recognition that wealth is often built over years, not days, and that patience is a virtue in the realm of financial growth. The disciplined individual understands the power of compound interest, the importance of delayed gratification, and the necessity of waiting for the right opportunities. This temporal awareness allows for strategic planning and the cultivation of resilience in the face of inevitable setbacks.

Moreover, discipline is about making informed choices and sticking to them. It involves setting clear financial goals and devising a roadmap to achieve them. These goals, whether they pertain to saving for retirement, investing in real estate, or building a diversified portfolio, require a disciplined approach to ensure they are met. It is the discipline that prevents deviation from the path, even when faced with tempting distractions or market volatility.

In the realm of wealth creation, discipline is also synonymous with self-control. It is the ability to curb impulsive spending, to resist the temptation of unnecessary luxuries, and to prioritize long-term financial health over immediate pleasure. This self-control is not about denying oneself but about making choices that align with one's financial objectives. It is about understanding the difference between wants and needs and aligning expenditures with values and priorities.

Additionally, discipline requires a commitment to continuous learning and adaptation. The financial world is dynamic, with ever-evolving markets, technologies, and economic conditions. A disciplined approach involves staying informed, seeking knowledge, and being willing to adjust strategies as circumstances change. This adaptability ensures that the disciplined individual remains on the cutting edge of financial trends, maximizing opportunities and minimizing risks.

Ultimately, discipline in wealth creation is about maintaining focus and determination. It is the inner strength that drives individuals to stick to their plans, to push through challenges, and to remain steadfast in their pursuit of financial independence. Through discipline, the abstract concept of wealth becomes tangible, a testament to the power of consistent and deliberate action. In this light, discipline is not merely a tool for wealth creation; it is the very foundation upon which financial success is built.

EMOTIONAL INTELLIGENCE

Navigating the intricate pathways of wealth creation requires not only a shrewd understanding of financial mechanisms but also a profound grasp of the human psyche. Emotional intelligence emerges as a pivotal attribute in this realm, serving as the bridge between shrewd financial acumen and sustainable wealth management. It is the subtle art of recognizing, understanding, and managing our own emotions, as well as perceiving and influencing the emotions of others. This skill becomes indispensable when making decisions that affect one's financial future.

In the high-stakes world of finance, emotions can often cloud judgment. Fear of loss, greed for gain, and the pressure of societal expectations can lead to impulsive decisions that might not align with long-term financial goals. Emotional intelligence equips individuals with the ability to stay grounded amidst these pressures. By fostering a heightened awareness of one's emotional triggers, individuals can cultivate a more rational approach to decision-making, ensuring that their choices are informed by logic rather than fleeting emotions.

Interpersonal relationships also play a crucial role in wealth creation. Whether it's negotiating a business deal, managing a team, or collaborating with partners, the ability to navigate social complexities with emotional intelligence can significantly impact success. This skill allows for effective communication, empathy, and conflict resolution, enabling individuals to build and maintain robust professional relationships. Understanding the emotional undercurrents in these interactions can lead to more fruitful collaborations and partnerships.

Moreover, emotional intelligence is instrumental in fostering resilience. The journey to wealth creation is fraught with challenges and setbacks. Those with high emotional intelligence are better equipped to handle failures and disappointments, viewing them as learning opportunities rather than insurmountable obstacles. This resilience is crucial for maintaining motivation and perseverance in the face of adversity.

Self-awareness, a core component of emotional intelligence, empowers individuals to identify their strengths and weaknesses. By understanding their own capabilities and limitations, they can make more informed decisions about where to allocate their resources and efforts. This introspective insight is invaluable for personal growth and strategic planning in wealth creation.

Furthermore, emotional intelligence enhances one's capacity for delayed gratification. In a world where instant results are often sought after, the ability to prioritize long-term benefits over immediate rewards can differentiate successful wealth creators from the rest. Emotional intelligence fosters patience and discipline, enabling individuals to stay focused on their long-term financial objectives.

In essence, emotional intelligence is not merely an adjunct to financial expertise but a fundamental pillar of it. It shapes the way individuals perceive and respond to the dynamic world of wealth creation, influencing their ability to make sound decisions, build lasting relationships, and persevere through challenges. By integrating emotional intelligence into their financial strategies, individuals can achieve a more holistic approach to wealth creation, one that balances the mind's analytical prowess with the heart's intuitive wisdom.

MAINTAINING A WEALTH MINDSET

In the ever-evolving realm of wealth creation, the mindset one cultivates is akin to the fertile soil from which the seeds of prosperity grow. It is an inner sanctuary, where thoughts and beliefs about wealth are nurtured, shaping the reality that unfolds. This mindset is not a stagnant entity, but a dynamic force that requires continual cultivation and vigilant maintenance to ensure it aligns with the principles of abundance and prosperity.

CHAPTER 10: THE PSYCHOLOGY OF WEALTH

The wealth mindset is characterized by an unwavering belief in one's ability to generate and sustain financial prosperity. It is not merely about accumulating monetary assets but understanding the flow of money as a tool to enhance life and create opportunities. Those who maintain this mindset perceive challenges as opportunities for growth, viewing setbacks not as failures but as valuable lessons that guide them to a more prosperous path.

A crucial aspect of maintaining a wealth mindset is the practice of gratitude. Recognizing and appreciating the abundance that already exists in one's life reinforces a positive outlook, attracting more wealth. This practice shifts focus from scarcity to abundance, transforming the way individuals interact with their financial environment. Gratitude acts as a magnet, drawing in more of what one appreciates, thereby amplifying wealth in all its forms.

Another vital element is the continuous pursuit of knowledge. Wealth-minded individuals understand that the financial landscape is ever-changing, and staying informed is paramount. By engaging with new ideas, investing in self-education, and seeking out mentors, one remains adaptable and open to innovative wealth-building strategies. This proactive approach ensures that the wealth mindset remains robust and resilient, capable of navigating the complexities of modern finance.

The company one keeps also plays a significant role in maintaining a wealth mindset. Surrounding oneself with like-minded individuals who share a commitment to growth and abundance fosters an environment of mutual support and inspiration.

These relationships serve as both a sounding board for new ideas and a source of motivation, propelling individuals toward their financial goals.

Moreover, maintaining a wealth mindset involves setting clear, intentional goals. These goals act as a roadmap, providing direction and purpose. They transform abstract desires into tangible objectives, allowing for focused effort and strategic planning. Regularly revisiting and adjusting these goals ensures alignment with one's evolving values and aspirations, keeping the wealth mindset attuned to personal growth and external circumstances.

Self-reflection is a powerful tool in this ongoing process. By assessing one's beliefs and attitudes towards money, individuals can identify and release limiting thoughts that hinder financial progress. This introspection fosters a deeper understanding of personal motivations and fears, paving the way for a more liberated and empowered approach to wealth creation.

Finally, maintaining a wealth mindset requires a balance between action and reflection. While proactive steps toward wealth accumulation are essential, equally important is the ability to pause, reflect, and recalibrate. This balance ensures that the pursuit of wealth remains aligned with one's core values, leading to a fulfilling and sustainable financial journey. In this dance between action and reflection, the wealth mindset is not only maintained but continually enriched, paving the way for a life of abundance and prosperity.

12

Chapter 11: Networking and Wealth

BUILDING RELATIONSHIPS

In the intricate tapestry of wealth creation, the threads of human connections are woven intricately, forming the foundation upon which financial growth is built. The art of building relationships is not merely an adjunct to financial success but a core component that enhances every other aspect of wealth creation. In the bustling marketplace of ideas and opportunities, relationships serve as the bridges that connect people to resources, information, and opportunities that might otherwise remain out of reach.

Picture a vast network of individuals, each with unique skills, knowledge, and experiences. This network is a living organism, constantly evolving and expanding. Within this ecosystem, the ability to forge meaningful connections can transform potential into reality. The process of building relationships begins with the simple yet profound act of reaching out. It is in these initial interactions that seeds of trust are sown, which, when nurtured, can blossom into fruitful alliances.

The nuances of effective relationship-building lie in the understanding of mutual benefit. It is not merely about what one can gain, but what one can offer. The most successful wealth creators approach relationships with a mindset of contribution, recognizing that value flows in both directions. This reciprocity is the lifeblood of strong connections, creating a synergy that propels both parties toward their goals.

In the realm of wealth creation, the power of relationships is amplified by the diversity of the network one cultivates. Diverse connections bring a wealth of perspectives and insights, sparking innovation and opening doors to unconventional paths. The ability to engage with individuals from varied backgrounds and industries enhances adaptability and resilience in the face of an ever-changing economic landscape.

Communication, the cornerstone of any relationship, must be approached with authenticity and empathy. Listening actively and expressing genuine interest in others' aspirations creates a foundation of respect and trust. In the digital age, where interactions often occur through screens, the challenge is to maintain a personal touch, ensuring that each connection feels valued and understood.

Mentorship is another vital aspect of relationship-building in the context of wealth creation. Learning from those who have traversed the path before brings invaluable insights and guidance. These mentors offer more than just advice; they become champions of one's journey, providing encouragement and opening doors to new opportunities.

Moreover, the relationships one builds are not confined to professional circles. Personal connections, family, and friendships also play a significant role in shaping one's financial journey. These relationships provide emotional support, grounding, and sometimes even the inspiration needed to pursue ambitious goals.

As one navigates the intricate dance of relationship-building, it is important to remember that the quality of connections often outweighs the quantity. Deep, meaningful relationships have the power to transcend transactional interactions, fostering a sense of community and belonging that enriches the wealth creation process.

In the end, the true wealth lies not just in financial success but in the rich network of relationships that support and sustain that success. Through the deliberate and thoughtful cultivation of these connections, one can unlock the full potential of wealth creation, transforming aspirations into tangible achievements.

MENTORSHIP AND GUIDANCE

In the realm of wealth creation, the influence of a mentor can be as profound as the strategies one might employ to amass financial success. A mentor serves as a beacon of wisdom, illuminating the path with insights gained through experience and offering guidance that is both practical and inspirational. The relationship between mentor and mentee is a dynamic interplay where learning transcends conventional boundaries, fostering growth that is both personal and financial.

The essence of mentorship lies not only in the transfer of knowledge but also in the cultivation of critical thinking and decision-making skills. A mentor, with their seasoned perspective, can provide invaluable insights into the complexities of financial markets, investment strategies, and risk management. They help demystify the intricate web of financial jargon and concepts, making them accessible and understandable. Through storytelling and sharing personal anecdotes, mentors bring to life the abstract principles of wealth creation, grounding them in reality.

Guidance from a mentor often extends beyond the technicalities of financial growth. It encompasses the shaping of attitudes and mindsets essential for long-term success. A mentor encourages resilience, patience, and perseverance, reinforcing the idea that wealth creation is not a sprint but a marathon. They instill a sense of discipline and the importance of continuous learning, traits that are crucial in navigating the ever-evolving financial landscape.

Moreover, mentors provide a network of connections, opening doors to opportunities that might otherwise remain out of reach. They introduce mentees to like-minded individuals, potential business partners, and industry experts, thus expanding their sphere of influence. This network becomes a valuable asset, offering support, advice, and collaboration possibilities that can significantly enhance one's wealth-building endeavors.

The guidance of a mentor is also crucial in helping individuals identify and harness their unique strengths. By recognizing and nurturing these strengths, mentors empower mentees to carve out a niche for themselves in the competitive world of finance. They encourage innovation and creativity, urging mentees to think outside the box and explore unconventional paths to success. This personalized approach ensures that the journey to wealth creation is not only effective but also aligned with the individual's values and aspirations.

In addition to one-on-one mentorship, guidance can also be sought from various platforms such as seminars, workshops, and online courses. These resources offer diverse perspectives and insights from multiple mentors, broadening one's understanding of wealth creation. Engaging with a community of learners and experts fosters a collaborative environment where ideas can be exchanged, and new strategies can be developed.

Ultimately, the role of mentorship and guidance in mastering wealth creation cannot be overstated. It is a catalyst for growth, providing the tools, knowledge, and support necessary to navigate the complexities of financial success. The wisdom imparted by mentors not only accelerates the journey towards wealth but also enriches it, ensuring that the pursuit of financial prosperity is as fulfilling as it is rewarding.

COLLABORATIVE VENTURES

In the intricate tapestry of wealth creation, collaborative ventures stand as a testament to the power of unity and shared vision. These ventures, often born from the synergy of diverse talents and resources, have the potential to transcend individual limitations and unlock unprecedented opportunities for financial growth. At the heart of collaborative ventures lies the principle that collective effort can yield results far greater than the sum of its parts. By pooling resources, knowledge, and expertise, individuals and organizations can navigate complex markets and seize opportunities that might otherwise remain out of reach. This approach not only diversifies risk but also enhances the potential for innovation and creativity, driving sustainable wealth creation.

The landscape of collaborative ventures is vast, encompassing partnerships, joint ventures, strategic alliances, and even informal networks of like-minded individuals. Each form carries its unique set of dynamics and requires careful consideration of goals, compatibility, and mutual benefit. Successful collaboration hinges on clear communication, trust, and a shared commitment to the venture's objectives. It is essential for all parties involved to align their interests and establish a framework for decision-making and conflict resolution.

One of the most significant advantages of collaborative ventures is the access to a broader pool of resources. This includes not only financial capital but also human capital, technological know-how, and market access. By combining these resources, collaborators can undertake projects of greater scale and complexity than they could individually. This access can be particularly beneficial in industries where the cost of entry is high or where rapid technological advancements require significant investment in research and development.

In addition to resource access, collaborative ventures foster innovation by bringing together diverse perspectives and expertise. The cross-pollination of ideas can lead to novel solutions and approaches that drive competitive advantage. This innovation is often crucial in rapidly evolving markets where adaptability and foresight are key to maintaining relevance and achieving long-term success.

While the benefits of collaborative ventures are substantial, they are not without challenges. Differences in organizational culture, management styles, and strategic priorities can pose significant hurdles. Effective collaboration requires a willingness to compromise and adapt, as well as mechanisms to manage and resolve disagreements. It is also essential to establish clear metrics for success and accountability to ensure that all parties remain committed to the venture's goals.

The digital age has further transformed the landscape of collaborative ventures, enabling new forms of partnership and cooperation across geographical boundaries. Technology facilitates seamless communication and data sharing, allowing collaborators to work together more efficiently and effectively. This has opened up opportunities for global partnerships that can tap into emerging markets and leverage diverse talent pools.

In the realm of wealth creation, collaborative ventures represent a powerful strategy for achieving growth and sustainability. By embracing the strengths and capabilities of others, individuals and organizations can navigate the complexities of the modern economy and harness the full potential of their combined efforts. As the world continues to evolve, the ability to collaborate effectively will remain a critical factor in mastering the art of wealth creation.

LEVERAGING SOCIAL CAPITAL

In the intricate tapestry of wealth creation, the threads of social capital are often the most overlooked yet profoundly influential. Social capital, unlike financial capital, is intangible. It comprises the networks of relationships among people who live and work in a particular society, enabling that society to function effectively. These networks, built on trust, mutual understanding, and shared values, serve as powerful catalysts for economic success and personal growth.

The essence of social capital lies in its ability to open doors that might otherwise remain closed. It functions as a bridge, connecting individuals to opportunities, resources, and information that are not readily accessible through conventional means. In the realm of wealth creation, these networks can be the difference between stagnation and exponential growth.

The formation of social capital begins with genuine interactions and the building of trust. It is not simply about amassing contacts but cultivating meaningful relationships that are mutually beneficial. This requires an investment of time and effort, as well as a sincere interest in the well-being of others. The reciprocity inherent in these relationships fosters a supportive environment where ideas can flourish and collaboration can thrive.

In professional settings, social capital can manifest in various ways. Mentorship, for instance, is a potent form of social capital. By seeking guidance from those with more experience, individuals can gain insights that accelerate their learning curve and help them avoid common pitfalls. Conversely, offering mentorship to others not only strengthens one's network but also enhances personal growth and leadership skills.

Furthermore, social capital plays a critical role in innovation and entrepreneurship. A diverse and well-connected network can provide access to a wealth of knowledge and expertise, enabling entrepreneurs to refine their ideas and bring them to fruition. The exchange of perspectives within a network can lead to the discovery of novel solutions and the identification of market opportunities that might otherwise go unnoticed.

In addition to fostering innovation, social capital also acts as a buffer during challenging times. A robust network can provide emotional support, practical advice, and even financial assistance in periods of adversity. This safety net can be crucial in maintaining resilience and finding pathways to recovery.

The impact of social capital extends beyond individual success; it also contributes to the collective prosperity of communities. Strong networks foster a sense of belonging and shared purpose, which can lead to collaborative efforts that benefit the wider society. Initiatives that address social issues, promote economic development, and enhance the quality of life are often born out of communities rich in social capital.

In the pursuit of wealth creation, the strategic cultivation of social capital is indispensable. By nurturing relationships and building trust within one's network, individuals can unlock opportunities that lead to sustainable success. Social capital, though intangible, is a powerful asset that enriches both the personal and professional spheres, paving the way for a more connected and prosperous future.

13

Chapter 12: Philanthropy and Giving Back

THE VALUE OF GIVING

In the quiet corners of our bustling world, there lies an often overlooked yet profoundly transformative force: the act of giving. It is a concept that transcends mere transactions and enters the realm of the soul, where the true essence of wealth creation is born. Unlike the tangible possessions we accumulate, giving is an intangible thread that weaves itself through the fabric of our lives, connecting us to one another in ways that no material wealth ever could.

Imagine a moment when you extended a helping hand to someone in need. Recall the warmth that enveloped you, a sensation far richer than the fleeting satisfaction of a purchase. This is the intrinsic value of giving, a value that cannot be measured in dollars or possessions but in the depth of human connection it fosters. When we give, we engage in a silent dialogue with the universe, declaring that we possess more than enough and are willing to share our abundance with others.

The act of giving liberates us from the shackles of materialism. It shifts our focus from what we lack to what we can offer, transforming our mindset from scarcity to abundance. This transformation is the cornerstone of true wealth creation, as it opens our eyes to the myriad ways in which we are already rich. By giving, we cultivate gratitude, and gratitude, in turn, becomes the fertile soil from which prosperity grows.

Moreover, giving is a catalyst for change, both within ourselves and in the world around us. It inspires a ripple effect, touching lives in ways we might never fully comprehend. A simple act of kindness can illuminate the darkest of days, offering hope and encouragement to those who might have lost their way. In this exchange, both the giver and the receiver are enriched, their lives intertwined in a dance of mutual benefit.

In the realm of wealth creation, giving is not merely a noble gesture; it is a strategic investment. It builds networks, strengthens communities, and fosters goodwill, all of which are invaluable assets in the pursuit of success. Those who understand the power of giving recognize that it is an essential component of any wealth-building strategy. They see beyond the immediate sacrifice and understand that the returns, though often intangible, are boundless.

As we navigate the complexities of modern life, it becomes increasingly clear that the accumulation of wealth is not the pinnacle of success. Rather, it is the ability to use that wealth to make a difference, to uplift others, and to leave a lasting impact on the world. In this light, giving becomes not just a moral obligation but a vital element of our legacy.

Thus, the value of giving extends far beyond the act itself. It is a reflection of our values, a testament to our humanity, and a guiding principle in the art of wealth creation. It reminds us that true prosperity is not measured by what we have but by what we give, and in that giving, we find the greatest treasure of all.

STRATEGIC PHILANTHROPY

In the realm of wealth creation, the concept of strategic philanthropy emerges as a compelling force that intertwines the pursuit of prosperity with the broader societal good. This approach to giving is not merely about the act of donation but involves a meticulously crafted plan that aligns philanthropic efforts with personal values and long-term financial goals. It represents a shift from traditional charitable contributions to a more impactful and sustainable method of fostering change.

Strategic philanthropy begins with the understanding that effective giving requires a clear vision and purpose. It involves identifying specific causes or issues that resonate deeply with the individual, allowing them to channel their resources toward areas where they can make the most significant difference. This intentional focus not only maximizes the impact of their contributions but also ensures that the philanthropic efforts are meaningful and fulfilling.

The process of strategic philanthropy often involves a thorough assessment of potential recipients, including charities, non-profit organizations, and community initiatives. This assessment is critical in determining the credibility and effectiveness of these entities in addressing the chosen cause. By conducting due diligence, individuals can ensure that their contributions are utilized efficiently and transparently, thereby enhancing the trust and reliability of their philanthropic endeavors.

Moreover, strategic philanthropy encourages the integration of philanthropy into one's overall financial planning. This integration allows individuals to leverage their financial acumen and resources to support their philanthropic objectives without compromising their financial security or future aspirations. By aligning charitable giving with investment strategies, individuals can create a sustainable model of philanthropy that grows alongside their wealth.

The impact of strategic philanthropy extends beyond the financial contributions themselves. It fosters a culture of giving that inspires others to participate, creating a ripple effect of positive change within communities and society at large. By setting an example of thoughtful and effective giving, individuals can influence others to consider their philanthropic impact, ultimately amplifying the reach and effectiveness of their efforts.

Furthermore, strategic philanthropy provides an opportunity for individuals to engage more deeply with the causes they support. It often involves forming partnerships with like-minded individuals and organizations, collaborating on initiatives, and actively participating in the development and implementation of solutions. This active involvement not only enhances the impact of their contributions but also enriches the individual's personal and professional growth.

As individuals navigate the complexities of wealth creation, strategic philanthropy offers a pathway to integrate their financial success with a commitment to social responsibility. It challenges them to think critically about the legacy they wish to leave behind and the difference they want to make in the world. By embracing strategic philanthropy, individuals can create a harmonious balance between accumulating wealth and contributing to the greater good, ultimately achieving a more fulfilling and purpose-driven life.

IMPACT INVESTING

As the world becomes increasingly interconnected and aware of global issues, a paradigm shift is occurring in how individuals and institutions approach investments. Impact investing emerges as a powerful strategy, aiming to generate not only financial returns but also positive social and environmental outcomes. This investment approach aligns with the growing consciousness about sustainable development and corporate responsibility, offering a compelling alternative to traditional investment strategies.

Impact investing is distinguished by its dual objective: achieving measurable social or environmental impact alongside financial gains. Unlike philanthropy, which is primarily driven by altruism without the expectation of financial returns, impact investing seeks to create value in a way that is both profitable and transformative. Investors in this space are motivated by the desire to contribute to solutions for pressing global challenges such as climate change, poverty alleviation, and access to education and healthcare.

The appeal of impact investing is further bolstered by the increasing evidence that investments with a focus on sustainability and social good can be competitive with, and sometimes outperform, conventional investments. This is attributed to several factors, including the growing consumer demand for ethically produced goods and services, regulatory incentives for sustainable practices, and the long-term benefits of mitigating risks associated with environmental and social issues.

One of the critical components of impact investing is the emphasis on measurable outcomes. Investors and fund managers employ various frameworks and tools to assess the impact of their investments. Metrics and standards such as the Global Impact Investing Network's (GIIN) IRIS+ system and the United Nations Sustainable Development Goals (SDGs) provide structured guidance for evaluating the efficacy and impact of investments. This rigorous approach ensures accountability and transparency, helping investors track progress and refine strategies to maximize impact.

The landscape of impact investing is diverse, encompassing a wide range of sectors and asset classes. Opportunities abound in areas like renewable energy, sustainable agriculture, affordable housing, and social enterprises, offering investors a chance to align their portfolios with their values. Additionally, the rise of impact-focused venture capital and private equity funds has made it easier for individuals and institutions to access these opportunities, contributing to the growth of the impact investing market.

Challenges remain, however, in the form of balancing financial returns with impact goals and addressing the potential for "impact washing," where investments are marketed as impactful without substantiated evidence. To navigate these challenges, investors must conduct thorough due diligence and engage with reputable fund managers who prioritize genuine impact and transparency.

In the evolving world of finance, impact investing represents a dynamic and promising avenue for those seeking to harness their capital for meaningful change. By integrating the pursuit of profit with the pursuit of positive outcomes, impact investing not only redefines the purpose of wealth creation but also fosters a more inclusive and sustainable global economy. As this field continues to mature, it holds the potential to reshape the investment landscape, driving innovation and fostering partnerships that address the critical issues facing humanity today.

CREATING A LEGACY

In the realm of wealth creation, the concept of legacy transcends mere financial success. It is an enduring imprint, a testament to one's values, vision, and the impact they leave on the world. Crafting a legacy involves a deep understanding of what one wishes to pass on, not just in terms of assets, but in terms of influence and inspiration. This pursuit is not solely about accumulation but about thoughtful distribution, ensuring that the benefits of one's hard work extend beyond personal gain.

A legacy is built on the foundation of intention. It requires clarity in defining the principles that guide decisions, both personal and financial. These principles serve as the compass, directing efforts towards endeavors that align with one's core beliefs and aspirations. The process of establishing a legacy begins with envisioning the future impact of present actions, considering how they might shape the lives of others and contribute to societal advancement.

Integral to legacy creation is the notion of stewardship. It is the responsibility of managing resources with foresight and care, ensuring their sustainability for future generations. This involves not only the prudent management of financial assets but also the nurturing of relationships and the cultivation of an enduring reputation. A legacy is enriched by the connections one forges, the mentorship offered, and the opportunities created for others to flourish.

Education plays a pivotal role in legacy building, both in terms of self-education and the education of others. By investing in knowledge, individuals equip themselves with the tools necessary to navigate the complexities of wealth management and to make informed decisions. Furthermore, by prioritizing the education of future generations, they ensure that the values and skills needed to sustain and build upon their legacy are passed down.

Philanthropy often emerges as a cornerstone in the architecture of a meaningful legacy. It embodies the commitment to give back to the community, to support causes that resonate with personal values, and to effect positive change. Strategic philanthropy is intentional and impactful, directed towards initiatives that promise long-term benefits and align with the legacy creator's vision for societal betterment.

Moreover, a legacy is not static; it evolves with time, adapting to changing circumstances and new insights. It is a dynamic construct, reflecting the growth and transformation of the individual and the world around them. As such, ongoing reflection and reassessment are necessary to ensure that the legacy remains relevant and impactful.

Ultimately, the essence of creating a legacy lies in its ability to inspire. It is not merely about what is left behind but about how it motivates others to pursue their own paths of significance. A well-crafted legacy serves as a beacon, guiding future generations towards a life of purpose and fulfillment, encouraging them to contribute meaningfully to the world. In this way, the legacy becomes a living entity, perpetuating the values and vision of its creator long after their time.

14

Chapter 13: Adapting to Economic Changes

ECONOMIC INDICATORS

Navigating the complex landscape of wealth creation requires a keen understanding of the various factors that influence economic health and prosperity. Among these, economic indicators stand as vital tools, offering insights into the economic environment that can greatly impact financial decisions. These indicators, often seen as the pulse of an economy, provide critical data that inform investors, policymakers, and business leaders about the current state and future trajectory of economic activity.

Economic indicators are broadly categorized into three types: leading, lagging, and coincident indicators. Leading indicators, such as stock market returns, manufacturing activity, and new business startups, are predictive in nature. They provide foresight into future economic conditions, allowing proactive adjustments in strategies for wealth creation. For instance, a rise in new building permits can signal upcoming growth in the housing market, prompting investors to seize opportunities in real estate or related sectors.

Lagging indicators, on the other hand, confirm trends after they have occurred. These include unemployment rates, corporate profits, and interest rates. While they may not provide early warnings, they offer validation of existing economic trends and reinforce decisions made based on leading indicators. For example, a decrease in unemployment rates, although lagging, can affirm a period of economic expansion, supporting continued investment in growth-oriented assets.

Coincident indicators, such as GDP and retail sales, move in tandem with the economy, offering a real-time snapshot of economic performance. These indicators are crucial for understanding current economic conditions and assessing the immediate impact of economic policies. Tracking GDP growth can guide investors in aligning their portfolios with the prevailing economic climate, ensuring their strategies are responsive to the present economic environment.

The interpretation of economic indicators requires not only an understanding of their individual significance but also an awareness of their interconnectedness. For example, an increase in consumer confidence, a leading indicator, can lead to higher retail sales, a coincident indicator, which in turn might lower unemployment, a lagging indicator. Recognizing these relationships enables a more comprehensive evaluation of economic conditions, facilitating informed decisions in wealth creation.

Furthermore, economic indicators are influenced by a multitude of factors, including monetary policy, fiscal policy, and global economic trends. Central banks, through their monetary policy, can impact interest rates and inflation, thereby affecting economic indicators like consumer spending and business investment. Similarly, government fiscal policies, such as taxation and public spending, can alter economic activity, influencing indicators such as GDP and employment levels.

In the global context, economic indicators can be affected by international trade dynamics, geopolitical events, and global market trends. Exchange rates, trade balances, and international investments are critical components that shape economic indicators and, consequently, wealth creation strategies. Understanding these global influences is paramount for investors seeking to navigate the complexities of international markets.

In essence, economic indicators are indispensable tools in mastering wealth creation. They offer a comprehensive view of economic conditions, enabling strategic decision-making that aligns with both current and anticipated economic realities. As such, a deep understanding of these indicators, coupled with an awareness of their broader economic implications, is essential for any individual or entity aiming to achieve sustained financial success in an ever-evolving economic landscape.

CHAPTER 13: ADAPTING TO ECONOMIC CHANGES

CRISIS MANAGEMENT

In the vast and tumultuous sea of wealth creation, navigating through crises can be likened to steering a ship through a storm. This subchapter delves into the art and science of crisis management, a crucial skill for anyone aspiring to master wealth creation. A crisis, whether financial, economic, or personal, often strikes without warning, challenging even the most seasoned wealth creators. The ability to manage such crises effectively can mean the difference between sinking and sailing through turbulent waters.

At the heart of crisis management is preparation. Just as a seasoned sailor anticipates storms and prepares accordingly, a successful wealth creator anticipates potential crises and develops strategies to mitigate their impact. This involves not only understanding the nature of potential crises but also developing a robust plan that includes contingency measures and risk assessment. Diversification of assets, maintaining liquidity, and having access to emergency funds are some of the key strategies to ensure resilience in the face of adversity.

Moreover, effective crisis management requires a calm and composed mindset. Panic and impulsive decisions can exacerbate the situation, leading to further losses. Instead, wealth creators should cultivate a mindset that embraces challenges as opportunities for growth and learning. This involves staying informed and making decisions based on data and analysis rather than emotions. By maintaining a clear perspective, wealth creators can identify the root causes of a crisis and develop tailored solutions.

Communication also plays a pivotal role in managing crises. Whether it's communicating with stakeholders, clients, or team members, clear and transparent communication can help in managing expectations and building trust. During a crisis, misinformation can spread quickly, leading to confusion and panic. Therefore, providing accurate and timely information can help in mitigating the impact of the crisis and maintaining stability.

Furthermore, learning from past crises is an essential aspect of crisis management. Each crisis, while challenging, offers valuable lessons that can strengthen future strategies. By analyzing past experiences, wealth creators can identify patterns and develop more robust systems to handle future challenges. This continuous learning process not only enhances crisis management skills but also contributes to overall growth and success in wealth creation.

In the realm of wealth creation, adaptability is another critical component of crisis management. The ability to adapt to changing circumstances and pivot strategies can turn potential setbacks into opportunities. This involves being open to new ideas, technologies, and methodologies that can enhance resilience and drive success. By fostering a culture of innovation and agility, wealth creators can navigate through crises with confidence and emerge stronger.

Ultimately, crisis management is an integral part of mastering wealth creation. It requires a proactive approach, strategic planning, effective communication, and a mindset geared towards continuous learning and adaptability. By honing these skills, wealth creators can not only weather the storms of crises but also harness their potential to propel them towards greater success and prosperity.

OPPORTUNITIES IN RECESSION

Recessions, often viewed as periods of economic downturn and uncertainty, can paradoxically present unique opportunities for wealth creation. During these times, the financial landscape undergoes significant shifts, creating openings for those with the foresight and courage to capitalize on them. Understanding the dynamics at play during a recession can empower individuals to make strategic decisions that may lead to substantial financial gains.

One of the primary opportunities during a recession is the potential for acquiring undervalued assets. As market confidence wanes, asset prices often fall, sometimes to levels well below their intrinsic value. For the astute investor, this presents a chance to purchase stocks, real estate, or other investments at a discount. The key is conducting thorough due diligence to identify assets that have been unduly punished by the broader market sentiment but retain strong fundamentals and long-term growth potential.

In addition to undervalued assets, recessions can lead to a realignment of consumer needs and preferences. Businesses that can pivot to meet these changing demands may find themselves in a position to thrive even as others struggle. For entrepreneurs, this means identifying gaps in the market created by the shifting economic landscape. Whether it's offering cost-effective alternatives to luxury goods or providing essential services that remain in demand, there are opportunities for innovation and growth.

Moreover, recessions often lead to increased availability of skilled labor at reduced costs. As companies downsize, a pool of talented individuals becomes available, eager to contribute to new ventures. For businesses looking to expand or improve their operations, this can be an ideal time to recruit top talent that might otherwise be unattainable. Leveraging this opportunity can enhance a company's competitive edge and position it for success when the economy rebounds.

During economic downturns, governments and central banks frequently implement measures to stimulate growth, such as lowering interest rates and introducing fiscal stimulus packages. These actions can create a favorable environment for borrowing and investing. Lower interest rates reduce the cost of capital, making it more affordable for businesses to finance expansion projects or for individuals to invest in income-generating assets. Understanding and utilizing these policy changes can be a critical component of a wealth creation strategy during a recession.

Furthermore, recessions can serve as a catalyst for personal financial discipline and strategic planning. With heightened awareness of financial vulnerability, individuals may be more motivated to reassess their spending habits, eliminate unnecessary expenses, and focus on building a robust financial cushion. This period of reflection and adjustment can lead to more sustainable wealth-building practices that endure beyond the recession itself.

While the challenges of a recession are undeniable, they also bring with them a set of opportunities that, if navigated wisely, can lead to substantial financial rewards. By staying informed, remaining adaptable, and maintaining a long-term perspective, individuals can not only weather the storm but also emerge from it with a stronger financial footing. Recessions, therefore, should not only be seen as periods of crisis but also as potential springboards for future prosperity.

LONG-TERM ECONOMIC TRENDS

The tapestry of wealth creation is intricately woven with the threads of long-term economic trends, which serve as both the backdrop and the driving force behind financial prosperity. These trends, often imperceptible in the short term, gradually shape the economic landscape over decades, influencing investment strategies, business decisions, and the accumulation of wealth. Understanding these trends is akin to deciphering the subtle shifts in the wind that guide the sails of a ship, steering it toward its destination.

At the heart of these long-term shifts are demographic changes. As populations age in developed countries, the economic implications are profound, affecting everything from labor markets to healthcare systems. The aging population trend leads to a decrease in the working-age population, which can slow economic growth and increase the burden on social security systems. Conversely, in emerging markets, youthful populations present opportunities for economic expansion, innovation, and consumer market growth. These demographic dynamics create a complex interplay that investors and policymakers must navigate to harness the potential for wealth creation.

Technological advancements are another cornerstone of long-term economic trends. The relentless march of technology has transformed industries, disrupted traditional business models, and created new avenues for wealth. The digital revolution, characterized by the rise of the internet, artificial intelligence, and automation, has reshaped the way businesses operate and interact with consumers. These innovations have not only increased productivity but also democratized access to information and opportunities, allowing individuals and small businesses to compete on a global scale. For those attuned to these technological shifts, the potential for wealth creation is boundless.

Globalization, while not a new phenomenon, continues to evolve and exert a significant impact on economic trends. The interconnectedness of global markets has facilitated trade, investment, and the flow of capital across borders. This has led to increased economic integration and interdependence among nations. However, globalization also brings challenges, such as trade imbalances and geopolitical tensions, which can create volatility in financial markets. Navigating this complex global landscape requires a keen understanding of the forces at play and the ability to adapt to changing circumstances.

Environmental sustainability is emerging as a critical long-term economic trend. As the world grapples with the impacts of climate change, the transition to a more sustainable economy is driving innovation and investment in green technologies and practices. This shift presents both challenges and opportunities for wealth creation. On one hand, industries that are slow to adapt may face regulatory pressures and reputational risks. On the other hand, those that embrace sustainability can unlock new markets and drive long-term growth. The integration of environmental considerations into economic decision-making is becoming increasingly important for investors seeking to build resilient and future-proof portfolios.

In the ever-evolving narrative of economic progress, these long-term trends serve as guiding stars. They provide context and direction, helping individuals and businesses to navigate the complexities of wealth creation in an uncertain world. By understanding and anticipating these trends, one can position themselves to capitalize on emerging opportunities and mitigate potential risks, ensuring a prosperous and sustainable financial future.

15

Chapter 14: The Journey to Mastery

CONTINUOUS LEARNING

In the realm of wealth creation, the ability to continuously learn is a fundamental pillar that distinguishes successful individuals from the rest. The landscape of financial prosperity is ever-evolving, characterized by rapid technological advancements, fluctuating market dynamics, and emerging economic trends. To navigate this complex environment, one must cultivate a mindset that embraces lifelong learning, adapting to new information and insights with agility and enthusiasm.

At the heart of continuous learning lies the recognition that knowledge is not a static asset but a dynamic resource that requires regular updating and refinement. This understanding compels individuals to actively seek out new knowledge, whether through formal education, self-directed study, or experiential learning. The pursuit of knowledge becomes a strategic endeavor, aimed at enhancing one's financial literacy, understanding of investment opportunities, and comprehension of economic principles.

The digital age has democratized access to information, providing a plethora of resources for those committed to expanding their financial acumen. Online courses, webinars, and financial blogs offer a wealth of insights into various aspects of wealth creation, from stock market strategies to real estate investment and beyond. Engaging with these resources allows individuals to stay informed about current trends and innovations, positioning themselves to capitalize on emerging opportunities.

Furthermore, continuous learning extends beyond the acquisition of technical knowledge. It encompasses the development of critical thinking skills, enabling individuals to analyze complex financial scenarios and make informed decisions. By honing these skills, one can assess risks and rewards with greater precision, thereby optimizing investment strategies and minimizing potential pitfalls.

In addition to self-education, learning from the experiences of others is invaluable. Networking with successful entrepreneurs, investors, and financial experts provides unique insights that textbooks and online courses cannot offer. These interactions often reveal practical wisdom and nuanced understanding of wealth creation that can significantly enhance one's financial journey.

Moreover, the practice of continuous learning fosters resilience in the face of financial setbacks. By maintaining a growth-oriented mindset, individuals are better equipped to adapt to changing circumstances, learn from failures, and persist in their pursuit of financial goals. This resilience is a critical component of long-term wealth creation, as it enables individuals to navigate economic downturns and capitalize on recovery periods.

Ultimately, continuous learning is not merely a strategy but a way of life for those committed to mastering wealth creation. It requires dedication, curiosity, and a willingness to challenge one's existing beliefs and assumptions. By cultivating a habit of lifelong learning, individuals can unlock new possibilities, innovate in their financial endeavors, and achieve sustainable prosperity. In this ever-changing world, the ability to learn, unlearn, and relearn is the key to staying ahead, ensuring that one's financial strategies remain relevant and effective in the pursuit of wealth.

ADAPTING TO CHANGE

In the intricate dance of wealth creation, change is an ever-present partner, demanding both attention and respect. It is a force that can either propel us forward or leave us behind, depending on how we respond to its rhythms. The world of finance and investment is a dynamic landscape, where the only constant is change itself. Mastering wealth creation requires not just an understanding of financial principles, but also an ability to adapt to the shifting tides of economic and social transformations.

The landscape of wealth creation is shaped by numerous factors, including technological advancements, geopolitical shifts, and evolving consumer behaviors. Each of these elements introduces new variables into the equation, making adaptability a crucial skill for anyone seeking to build and sustain wealth. As new technologies emerge, they redefine industries and create opportunities that were previously unimaginable. The rise of digital currencies, for instance, has disrupted traditional banking systems and introduced a new realm of investment possibilities. Those who can swiftly adapt to these innovations are often the ones who can capitalize on them most effectively.

Geopolitical changes, such as trade agreements or conflicts, can have profound impacts on markets and investment strategies. Savvy wealth creators monitor global events closely, understanding that shifts in political landscapes can lead to new risks and opportunities. For example, a change in trade policies can affect the supply chains of multinational corporations, influencing stock prices and opening doors for strategic investments in alternative markets.

Consumer behaviors are another critical component of the wealth creation puzzle. As societal values evolve, so too do spending habits and investment trends. The growing emphasis on sustainability and social responsibility has led to the rise of ethical investing, where individuals and institutions prioritize investments in companies that align with their values. This shift reflects a broader change in how wealth is perceived and utilized in today's world, highlighting the need for adaptability in investment approaches.

Adapting to change also involves a psychological component. It requires a mindset that is open to learning and growth, even in the face of uncertainty. This mindset is characterized by resilience, flexibility, and a willingness to take calculated risks. Successful wealth creators cultivate a sense of curiosity and a desire to continuously expand their knowledge, recognizing that the ability to adapt is as much about mindset as it is about strategy.

In the realm of wealth creation, those who thrive are often those who can anticipate change and position themselves to benefit from it. This involves not only reacting to current events but also forecasting future trends and preparing for them. By developing a keen sense of awareness and a proactive approach, individuals can navigate the complexities of the financial world with confidence and foresight.

Ultimately, adapting to change is not just a survival mechanism; it is a pathway to innovation and growth. It allows wealth creators to transform challenges into opportunities and to remain resilient in the face of adversity. In a world where change is inevitable, mastering the art of adaptation is essential for achieving lasting success in wealth creation.

CELEBRATING SUCCESS

The vibrant hues of achievement paint an exquisite canvas in the realm of wealth creation. It is within this dynamic landscape that the fruits of labor, strategy, and perseverance come to life, revealing a tapestry woven with the threads of dedication and innovation. Each milestone reached and every goal surpassed becomes a testament to the human spirit's relentless pursuit of prosperity.

CHAPTER 14: THE JOURNEY TO MASTERY

In the world of wealth creation, celebrating success is not merely an act of acknowledgment; it is a vital component in the cycle of growth and motivation. The triumphs, whether grand or modest, serve as beacons of hope and inspiration, illuminating the path for further endeavors. They are the moments when the abstract dreams of financial independence crystallize into tangible reality, offering a glimpse of the potential that lies ahead.

As one stands at the pinnacle of a hard-earned victory, the air is charged with a sense of accomplishment. The journey to success is often fraught with challenges and obstacles, making each victory even sweeter. It is a time to reflect on the strategies that propelled one forward, the lessons learned along the way, and the resilience that fortified the spirit against adversity. This reflection is not only a personal exercise but also a beacon for others who aspire to walk a similar path.

The celebration of success in wealth creation often extends beyond personal satisfaction. It becomes a communal affair, where mentors, partners, and supporters gather to share in the joy. The bonds forged in the crucible of ambition are strengthened in these moments of shared triumph. Such celebrations foster a culture of encouragement and collaboration, where the success of one is seen as the success of all.

Moreover, recognizing achievements serves as a catalyst for continued ambition. It fuels the desire to set new goals, to push boundaries, and to explore uncharted territories. The euphoria of success ignites a spark that drives innovation and creativity, encouraging individuals to envision possibilities beyond the horizon. It is this relentless pursuit of excellence that propels the cycle of wealth creation forward, ensuring that the journey is ever-evolving and the destination ever-expanding.

Yet, amidst the celebrations, there is a profound understanding that success is not an endpoint but a milestone. It is a reminder of the potential that lies within and the possibilities that await. As the champagne glasses clink and the accolades flow, there is a quiet resolve to remain steadfast in the pursuit of greater achievements. The celebration, therefore, becomes a moment of rejuvenation, a pause that refreshes the spirit before embarking on the next phase of the wealth creation journey.

In the grand tapestry of wealth creation, celebrating success is an art form in itself. It is the harmonious blend of gratitude, reflection, and aspiration that transforms achievements into stepping stones for future endeavors. As the narrative of wealth creation unfolds, these moments of celebration become the cherished anecdotes that inspire generations to come, reminding them of the power of vision, the strength of determination, and the boundless possibilities that await those who dare to dream.

INSPIRING OTHERS

The art of wealth creation extends beyond personal accumulation; it encompasses the ability to inspire others to pursue their own paths to prosperity. Within the intricate tapestry of financial success, there lies a profound power in motivating those around us to recognize and harness their potential. This power is not merely about sharing strategies or offering advice, but about igniting a spark that encourages others to envision a brighter future for themselves.

Imagine a mentor whose words resonate deeply, whose actions speak louder than any financial statement. This individual does not simply preach the mechanics of wealth building, but embodies the principles through genuine living. They weave stories of their own trials and triumphs, painting vivid pictures of resilience and determination. Through their narrative, they reveal not just the destination but the winding road that led them there, complete with all its challenges and victories.

In a world where financial literacy often feels like a distant concept, the ability to demystify complex ideas is invaluable. This ability transforms abstract notions into tangible realities. Those who inspire others in wealth creation break down barriers, making concepts accessible and relatable. They bridge the gap between aspiration and achievement, showing that wealth is not an exclusive privilege but an attainable goal for all who dare to pursue it.

The essence of inspiring others lies in the authenticity of one's message. It is not enough to simply tell others what they should do; the real impact comes from showing them how it can be done. This involves sharing personal experiences, admitting failures, and celebrating successes in equal measure. This transparency fosters trust and credibility, empowering others to believe in the possibility of their own success.

Moreover, the ripple effect of inspiration can transform entire communities. When one person is inspired to seek wealth, they often bring others along on their journey. Families, friends, and colleagues become part of a collective movement toward financial empowerment. This communal pursuit creates a supportive environment where individuals uplift one another, fostering a culture of growth and innovation.

Inspiring others is not a one-time act but a continuous commitment to nurturing potential. It requires patience, empathy, and an unwavering belief in the capabilities of those around us. It is about planting seeds of encouragement and providing the nourishment needed for them to flourish. Whether through mentorship, education, or simply leading by example, the impact of inspiring others can resonate for generations.

As the cycle of inspiration perpetuates, it transforms the landscape of wealth creation. It shifts the focus from individual gain to collective prosperity, emphasizing the importance of collaboration and shared success. In this way, inspiring others becomes a cornerstone of mastering wealth creation, ensuring that the journey toward financial abundance is not a solitary endeavor but a shared adventure filled with possibility and promise.

16

RECOMMENDED BOOKS

POOR DAD RICH DAD
THE PSYCHOLOGY OF MONEY

www.ingramcontent.com/pod-product-compliance
Lightning Source LLC
Chambersburg PA
CBHW050259230526
45471CB00005B/1950